THE FLAG IN THE WIND

THE FLAG IN THE WIND

The Story of the National Movement in Scotland

by

J. M. MacCORMICK

BIRLINN

This edition published in 2008 by
Birlinn Limited
West Newington House
10 Newington Road
Edinburgh EH9 1QS

www.birlinn.co.uk

First published in 1955 by Victor Gollancz Ltd, London

ISBN: 978 1 84158 780 6

British Library Cataloguing-in-Publication Data
A catalogue record for this book is available from the British Library

Printed and bound in Great Britain by CPI Cox & Wyman, Reading, RG1 8EX

FOREWORD

Remember John MacCormick

In 1948 I was demobilized from the armed Forces and was looking for inspiration. I found it in John MacCormick.

I met him in the street and with the boldness of youth stopped him and gave him my views. He gave me his. Soon I was lying in wait for him. Then I became a visitor to his house. He was a dreamer and so was I. Above all we dreamed of a Scotland with its old self confidence. He financed the Stone of Destiny foray and tended its aftermath. That was a minor symbolic gesture. Our next one was the Queen's Title action of 1953. We dreamed it up one spring day on the banks of Loch Lomond.

When George VI died his daughter took Elizabeth II as her title. There never had been a first Elizabeth, except in England, and 'the numeral' gave great offence. It suggested that Scotland had been incorporated into England. The Stone of Destiny had brought us to the public's attention and they looked to us for leadership. John and I raised an action in the Court of Session seeking to interdict the Queen from calling herself 'Elizabeth II'. So far as the title went we failed. Instead we got a judgment about the nature of the Union which went far further than we had hoped. Lord Cooper, the Lord President of the Court of Session said,

> . . . considering that the union legislation extinguished the Parliaments of Scotland and of England and replaced them with a new parliament, I have difficulty in seeing why it should have been supposed that the new Parliament of Great Britain must inherit all the peculiar characteristics of the

English Parliament but none of the Scottish Parliament as if all that happened in 1707 was that . . . Scottish representatives were admitted to the Parliament of England. That is not what was done.

In short, Scotland had not been incorporated into England. This doesn't seem much today. In 1953 it was revolutionary. It was what John and a few others had been saying for twenty-five years. It was a victory. Another was to follow.

A year later, on being called to the Scottish bar, I had to swear allegiance to the Crown, I refused to take the oath 'in proper form', that is to Elizabeth II. I was told that if I didn't I could never become an advocate. It was a bitter, lonely time. It took more courage than anything I did at Westminster Abbey. I stuck it out until they backed down. The Queen's title in Scotland became Elizabeth without the appendage of a numeral and has remained so ever since. What we failed to get in our legal action we now had won elsewhere. In 1954 this was a step too far. The great in the land felt that a divine institution had been tarnished and its power in some way diminished. A human sacrifice was needed.

The Royalists closed ranks. They sent me to Coventry but I survived. They turned on John. He was sacked from his partnership in the law firm he had founded. He had known of this risk and had chosen to run it. He applied to join the bar where I was already fighting for survival. In the vast portfolio of learning then required for entrance to the Faculty of Advocates he lacked one minor examination pass. It was within the power of the Dean of Faculty to grant an exemption which John, an established and distinguished lawyer, had every reason to expect. Alas the Dean too had recently been advocating reform in the Scottish constitution. If he were thought to be favouring John MacCormick he might never be made a judge. He refused the dispensation. Moreover he intimated that John would have to attend classes before he could sit the required examination. As John had until recently been Rector of Glasgow University this was a deliberate attempt at a petty humiliation. It was beyond endurance. He was left jobless. He died broken in health, but not in spirit, a few years later. I miss him still.

Sixty and more years ago there were few people who stood up for Scotland. The Stone itself might have been the end of John yet he took the risk. We both knew there was even greater risk in attacking royalty. I was young and would survive, but John was middle-aged with a family to support. The great and the good feared him as a danger to their mediocrity. They smothered him to death.

His son Neil describes elsewhere in these pages how John was a good father to his children. He was much more than that. He was father to the Scottish nation we know today.

Remember John MacCormick

Ian Hamilton
August 2008

INTRODUCTION

JOHN MACCORMICK WAS BORN in 1904 and died in 1961. Through his short life's work, he contributed greatly to transforming Scots' self-understanding of their own country and its potential place in the world. There were two main phases of this. The first ran from 1928 through till 1942, when he played a decisive part in establishing first the National Party of Scotland (1928–34)[1] and then, by merger with the Scottish Party, the Scottish National Party, which has since 2007 become the governing party in the Scottish Parliament. This indeed represents a massive growth from the condition of the still rather small and electorally unsuccessful SNP of the 1930s.

The second phase followed a schism in the SNP in 1942, with the subsequent foundation by John MacCormick and his associates of the Scottish Convention as an all-party and non-party umbrella organisation for Scottish Home Rule. After the end of the 1939–45 war, the Convention organised a series of widely representative Scottish National Assemblies, and at the 1949 Assembly, the 'Scottish Covenant' was launched. This was an engagement among its signatories to do 'all within our power' to secure a re-established Scottish Parliament for Scottish affairs, and it achieved within two years signatures from something approaching two thirds of the Scottish electorate. This was a remarkable feat of consciousness-raising, though it was not immediately effective in prompting more

---

1 The new Appendix added to this edition gives fascinating evidence of the reasons that moved MacCormick's commitment to establishing the National Party in 1928.

than a considerable expansion of administrative devolution to the Scottish Office.

Two high-visibility events occurred during and in the aftermath of the main Covenant campaign. One was the removal of the Stone of Destiny from Westminster, in which MacCormick played a significant part, especially after the arrival of the Stone in Scotland. The second, in 1952–3, was the challenge mounted to the numeral 'II' chosen for the title of the new Queen, Elizabeth, on the death of her father, George VI, in 1952. The challenge to this by MacCormick and Ian Hamilton in the Court of Session, and the celebrated judgment by Lord Cooper in *MacCormick v Lord Advocate,* shook to the core prevailing British constitutional theory. It raised real doubts about the absolute sovereignty of Parliament in light of the potentially binding effect of the Treaty of Union of 1707 in its provisions in favour of Scottish laws and institutions. The case remains after fifty years a landmark in our constitutional law and history.

These – together with the election of MacCormick as Rector of the University of Glasgow in 1950 – are highlights of this book, *The Flag in the Wind.* It needs no extended introduction to lead the reader into MacCormick's own account of them. What may be more to the point is to say a little about what manner of man this was. I come to the task in the privileged but also partial position of being his son – my parents had four children, Iain, me, Marion and Elspeth, and because of the early death of his brother Donnie, a fellow nationalist, our father became a closely involved uncle to cousins Donald and Alistair also. Especially during family holidays, we functioned to a large extent as a family of six siblings.

We were a happy family. My mother, Margaret Miller, was a tower of strength to us all, and created space in which, for all his huge workload between his legal practice and his politics, my father remained a very engaged dad to his children. The incidence of two world wars made us an extended family with three aunts unmarried and one widowed. My maternal grandmother lived in a large house in Bothwell with a huge garden. There we ran wild during weekends, and in those parts of the school summer holidays when we were not away for a month in Bunessan in Mull or Killin in Perthshire or at the long-term favourite holiday place of Tayvallich in mid-Argyll. Dad made kites and flew them with us, once bringing down the telephone wires as a consequence of over-zealousness. He made balsa-wood gliders and taught us how to make more elaborate planes from kits you could buy in Glasgow's Argyll Arcade. We had terrific games with toy soldiers and spring-cannons that could fire wire nails at lead soldiers without danger to boyish eyes or limbs. We went on picnics to Loch Lomond or Loch Lubnaig or Inverkip in summer weekends, being fortunate in possession of a car, usually a rather rickety one, in the years of Hitler's war and the ten that followed it. Above all, there were boats – three beautifully made model yachts devised and built by Dad, and rowing boats that we rented along with the holiday house when we were in Mull or Tayvallich, and in which we learned to be safe boat people and to be self-reliant in the rough waters of Loch Sween or Loch na Lathaich.

Our large double top flat home at 2 Park Quadrant in Glasgow's Park district overlooked Kelvingrove Park towards the magnificent side view of Gilbert Scott's Glasgow University. Beyond lay the Kilpatrick and Campsie Hills and the more distant Argyll and Perthshire mountains, with cityscape and Clydeside cranes in the middle foreground. Scotland in miniature, I have often subsequently thought. Not inappropriately so, for my father's deepest commitments were always to Scotland – the people, the history, the philosophy and poetry, the land and landscape (of which for a while he showed himself a more than competent amateur painter). Home was both a political base with phone often ringing, and a place of hospitality both to political friends and associates and to the extended family. So there was always surrounding talk and often a buzz of excitement about whatever was current in the news and whatever the Covenanters were currently agitating about – the closure of Clyde piers, or of West Lothian shale oil, for example. If you were a small boy or young teenager interested in political affairs, simply assuming the role of an unobtrusive listener gave a great political education in a very particular kind of politics.

Despite his justified public reputation for being the douce and impassive Glasgow lawyer, the master of compromise in committee and a pursuer of the practical rather than the ideal, a gradualist rather than a fundamentalist in his approach to Scottish self-government, MacCormick was a romantic in his soul, a lover of philosophy and poetry, fascinated in the history of his country. He was very much of Gaelic Scotland in family background, though boyhood in Stepps and education there and at Woodside School in Glasgow made him also appreciate the lowland Scot, as he did all the more after marriage to Margaret Miller. He wrote occasional poetry all his life and even, long before their political fall-out, had an encouraging correspondence with C M Grieve (Hugh MacDiarmid) about some of his youthful poems. One of these, in Scots, for which he had a particular penchant himself was about his sense of a personal destiny, and has a strong ring of Calvinism in it. This was despite his own renunciation of the Church, whose creed he could not recite with honesty though he remained deeply monotheistic in attitude and very much a subscriber to liberal Christian ethics – but he was much more a liberal than anything else in his world view. There may be more of Kant than of Calvin here:

I dinna fear the storm,
For the wind can speak tae me
O' a life that has nae form
But my ain stramasherie.

I dinna fear the daurk
For the nicht is kind tae me
Wha hae done sic fearsome wark
As I'd gar nae man tae see.

I'm no afeart o' God,
Though He kens a' things, they say,
And in his fist he'll haud
Our doom on judgement day.

But aye I fear mysel',
For in me there's a voice
Coming from Heaven or Hell –
I canna tak my choice.

His sense of being driven by the inner 'voice' made him decisive and even on occasion headstrong, despite the lawyerish aspect of his reputation. To read of the moment of schism at the SNP Annual Conference in Edinburgh in 1942 is to be transported to a high moment of anger and emotion and a decision welling out of pent-up frustration. Again, to read of the decision he took in cold blood to assist the highly risky venture of trying to take the Stone of Destiny from Westminster and then the cloak-and-dagger part he played in the aftermath of its success is to see somebody willing to take high risks in the cause of what by his own voice was right, regardless of personal consequences. The same was true in the narrow world of Glasgow solicitors' practice when it came to challenging the establishment over the Queen's title, not just as a matter of political judgement but also at the level of fundamental constitutional law. These adventures in the end cost him his partnership in the firm Stewarts Nicol

MacCormick and Co., which he had founded originally on his own and subsequently by amalgamation in 1947 with two other practices in Glasgow. His attempt to be admitted as an advocate at the Scottish bar in Edinburgh after doing the required 'year of idleness' was rejected by the Faculty of Advocates. The Dean of Faculty refused to waive any of the examination requirements in favour even of an established and obviously highly competent courtroom lawyer – a competence that had been strikingly revealed when he argued his own case as leading petitioner in *MacCormick v Lord Advocate*. Some commentators and historians have written slightingly of MacCormick in comparison with other figures of prominence in the national movement. It seems doubtful, however, if any of the others paid a price in terms of personal fortune remotely equivalent to that he paid for following his voice.

So an account of the man has to include a judgement about his courage and readiness to face adversity, and should acknowledge that these were formidable. This also involved courage in the face of pain, for he suffered throughout his adult life from painful and occasionally agonising stones in the kidney, and also in his last years from a very irritating form of dermatitis. The stones in the kidney could be partly alleviated by a citric acid-based lemon cordial that brother Iain used to make for general use in the house. But latterly at least MacCormick resorted more and more to alcohol as a necessary analgesic for the sheer pain he suffered, and the combined effect of liver and kidney disease carried him away in mid 1961 just before his fifty-seventh birthday. As his friend Professor Andrew Dewar Gibb said in his eulogy at the funeral in Glasgow University War Memorial Chapel, he was a man of rare courage in the face of illness and pain, who frequently went out campaigning and addressing meetings when others would have taken to a hospital bed. Dewar Gibb also said this in conclusion of his address:

John MacCormick has . . . gone from amongst us, but he has
left his name indelibly written in the history of the country
he loved so devotedly.

This is not the place or the time to speculate whether his
opinions will prevail or fail utterly. But of this I am sure. If
in time to come a new and different Scotland comes to be
erected, the work and the name of John MacCormick will be
in it as the headstone in the corner.

Well, a different Scotland has been erected. We live in new
times in the twenty-first century. Since 1999, we have had a
Scottish Parliament sitting in Edinburgh, still as a 'home rule'
or 'devolved' parliament, yet even as such a transformational
force in our society and indeed, in its very being, an
expression of a transformed self-understanding of Scotland
and its people. Since May 2007, the Scottish National Party
under the leadership of First Minister Alex Salmond has
formed the government in that parliament, and over its first
year in office made great progress in the judgement of most
observers of the Scottish scene. The contrast with October
1961 is a striking one.

It has certainly turned out that both the political ventures
on which John MacCormick embarked were essential
forerunners of the journey Scotland took since his death. The
Scottish Parliament would not have come into being without
a strong cross-party commitment to the project, such as
achieved through the 'Constitutional Convention' established
in 1988. Probably without the external catalyst of, and potential
threat from, the Scottish National Party, the Convention
itself might not have sufficed. And certainly, when it came to
the referendum campaign of 1997, it was vital that the SNP
brought its full weight in with Liberal Democrats, Labour
and non-aligned forces to secure the greatest possible – and a
more than adequate – majority for establishing a parliament
with some tax-varying powers, and with full-hearted popular

support behind it. Truly, it took both what one might call the 'Covenant tendency' as represented in the Convention, and the 'SNP tendency' as represented in the clear stand-out for a more fundamental long-term solution, to bring about the first great transformation of Scotland's place in the UK and the wider world since 1707.

Moreover, the reader of *Flag in the Wind* who attends to the appendix containing the Covenant association's 'Blueprint for Scotland' will there discover a document that remarkably prefigures a great deal of what is in the Scotland Act 1998, the constituent charter of the current Scottish Parliament. What the Covenanters envisaged and asked for in 1949–51 is more or less what Scotland eventually got in 1999. In that respect, the concluding prophecy of *The Flag in the Wind* has been fulfilled, albeit over a longer stretch of time than its author foretold:

> Flags as well as straws show the way the wind is blowing. Movements of the spirit, springing from the most deeply rooted sentiments of the people, can never be denied their goal. There is no doubt in my mind that long before the end of this century the Parliament of Scotland will once more be opened with ancient pomp and ceremony and that in this new age the representatives of her people will make her a valued partner in the British Commonwealth and an ideal ground for experiments in human progress. The promise implicit in her long history will yet be fulfilled.

I add only two remarks: I was deeply proud to attend that ceremonial opening as one of Scotland's then Members of the European Parliament. Dad would have been pleased, too,[2] for after 1958 he came to see that the European Community (now 'Union') was another theatre, additional to that of the

2 Not, however, quite as pleased (I think) as he would have been over Iain's election as SNP MP for Argyll, 1974–79.

Commonwealth, in which Scotland had a role to play that would eventually be taken, as taking it we now are.

The Flag in the Wind is an inspiring read for all who rejoice in Scotland's new flourishing in circumstances of a partial self-government that seems destined to extend itself steadily further. It expresses the vision of one man, who was indeed one among many, but for a time foremost of the many, who foresaw the possibility and did much to make it an actuality. He was a fine man and this is a fine book.

Neil MacCormick
August 2008

PREFACE

In the pages which follow I have told the story of the growth of the National Movement in Scotland from the time of the foundation of the National Party in 1928 down to the end of 1954. In writing it, however, I have done so deliberately from a personal point of view, believing not only that it would thus be of greater general interest but also that it would have been impossible for one of the main participants in the events described to do otherwise with fairness. It would have been foolish to try to maintain an appearance of objective impartiality which I could not genuinely feel.

It therefore follows that what I have written cannot be an exhaustive history of the movement. For example, since I resigned from the Scottish National Party in 1942, I have known no more about its internal development than any other outsider and I could not pretend to tell its story, or expound its present aims and policies.

It also follows that I have depended largely on personal recollection and while I believe that all my facts and dates are correct I apologize in advance if anyone should complain of error.

Because I believe that my theme is more than solely of Scottish interest I hope that my book will find English as well as Scottish readers. Apart altogether from any question of Scottish nationalism, there is a fundamental matter in the political development of the United Kingdom which should give cause for wide concern—that is the increasing rigidity of our two major political parties, their almost complete joint monopoly of the modern means of public communication, and the powerful discipline which they are able to impose upon their members. The growth of any considerable minority is so handicapped as to be almost impossible, and yet it is only through growing minorities that beneficial changes can come.

The rise of the national movement in Scotland during the last thirty years from very small beginnings to the point now where it can exercise at least some visible influence on the policies of the two parties is, therefore, a matter of encouragement for all who would preserve the good health of democracy. It is a story of a very small David battling with two Goliaths and slowly pushing them against their will in the way he wishes to go.

My thanks are due to the publishers of the *Economist* and of the *Scotsman* for permission to reprint the articles which appear in the Appendices.

J. M. M.

CHAPTER ONE

IN ONE OF HIS letters Robert Burns spoke of the "strong tide of Scottish prejudice" which flowed in his veins. I suppose that most of the ideals which we cherish and rationalise derive their first strength from some such tide of prejudice. For my own part, I cannot remember any time even in my childhood when I was not conscious of a strong feeling of pride in Scotland and of at least a vaguely realised idea that somehow my own country had been thwarted in the fulfilment of her destiny. Events recorded in school history books which seemed in no way to disturb my classmates or my teachers caused in me an uneasy resentment. When I read of the Saxon Princess Margaret who fled from the Norman Conquest and married the Scottish King Malcolm Canmore I thought of her as an overbearing prig rather than as the Saint she afterwards became. She certainly seems completely to have dominated her husband. Nearly all their sons were given Saxon rather than Celtic names. Her refusal or her inability to learn the Celtic language of her husband's court and her introduction of hordes of English churchmen to Romanise the Celtic Church, laid the foundations of that extraordinary myth which centuries later was to justify a false feeling of racial division among the Scottish people.

I disliked intensely the Norman adventurers whom Margaret's son David introduced into Scotland and with thorough partisanship I completely disbelieved the statements of historians that many of our greatest Scottish families were descended from them. I was a firm adherent of the theory that both the Bruces and the Stewarts were of

Highland origin and I can remember the pleasure with which I learned that even Shakespeare in *Macbeth* accepted as true the story that the Stewarts were descended from the chiefs of Lochaber.

I find it difficult to discover any personal reason for this early development of Scottish sentiment. My father and mother were both Gaelic-speaking Highlanders but the history books which in those days were purveyed in Scottish schools regarded the Highlanders as only recently emerged from utter savagery and had invented the "Scotchman" who was just a northern Englishman in disguise.

Certainly at home I was taught a proper pride in race and I can still recite the genealogy of all four of my grandparents back for many generations, but the race to which I belonged was dispossessed and the Scotland of which I read in school was not my people's inheritance.

I must, therefore, frankly admit that my earliest notions about Scotland were quite irrational and that all my life I have been biased towards a view of Scottish nationhood which is inconsistent both with her present position in the United Kingdom and with the idea, until recently so prevalent, that Scotland was just another like the kingdoms of the Heptarchy which had been merely laggard in uniting with the rest.

There is something to be said for the belief that at the right time and in the right place ideas enter men's minds from a collective unconscious. There is a unity of purpose behind the diverse actions of men working sometimes inexorably towards a goal which has been felt rather than foreseen by those who move towards it. What I sensed as a child, what seemed to be a personal and private reaction to events, was, in fact, a symptom of a widespread change of spirit which was taking place all over Scotland in the early years of the twentieth century.

The change was at first manifested in a new reading of our history. The work of men like Principal Rait of Glasgow University and Professor Watson of Edinburgh showed that the nineteenth-century conception of a divided Scotland was wrong. The evidence of place-names, of folk-lore, of tradition and of recorded fact all pointed to a new idea, that the essential core of the Scottish people had remained racially unchanged through all the centuries since Calgacus had defied the Roman legions of Agricola. True, there had been importations from many sources, especially among the aristocracy. Equally true, the dominant language in a great part of the Lowlands changed slowly through the centuries from Gaelic to an Anglican dialect. Yet so strong was the memory of racial unity that many years after Gaelic was forgotten in the south-eastern districts it was still commonly called *lingua materna*, the mother tongue. There were many feuds and divisions, internecine strife and sometimes civil war, but these were the symptoms not of racial diversity but of political and religious faction. Time and again, when the essence of the nation's life was threatened by conquest, unity was recovered and men of north and south, of east and west marched together to defend their own.

The rediscovery of a sense of common purpose and essential unity was the necessary prelude to a national reawakening. It was followed soon by a new budding of literature, of art and of music, the expression however individual in its terms of a new consciousness of national identity.

At first thought, it might well seem surprising that such an awareness of nationhood should come to life in Scotland after more than 200 years of close union with England. The Treaty of Union of 1707 which amalgamated the Parliaments of the two countries had as its avowed object the merging of the two kingdoms till they should be indistinguishably one, and during a large part of the nineteenth century it looked as though the object might be achieved. After the Napoleonic wars Scotland settled down to the business of getting rich quick. Parliament and government were far away in London, but their functions in those days were not such as to make them much felt in the economic and social life of the people. The politics of Church government were of far more immediate and direct concern to the ordinary man than were the politics of the United Kingdom. Sentimental pride in the achievements of Scottish regiments in the Imperial wars was a sufficient sop to an uneasy national conscience and, in any case, if it could not be proved it could, at least, be asserted that the Scot was just a different kind of Englishman. North Britain became the postal appellation of Scotland and seemed to be a suitable name for a country which had become a mere province of its neighbour.

Yet, out of almost imperceptible beginnings, an immense change has already taken place, a change which has affected all classes of the people and which, whatever its final outcome, is bound to influence the future political development not only of Scotland but also of the British Isles, and the Empire and perhaps of Europe as well. For better or for worse, the experiment which began in 1707, of completely fusing two distinct nations and making them one, has failed and now the task of statesmanship is to devise a new and better form of Union which will not deny to either party the right to be itself.

That the rebirth of national self-respect which is summed up in the change of Scotch back to Scots should give rise to the development of a national movement aiming at some measure of self-government was inevitable and it is with the growth of that movement that I am concerned in this book. I have myself grown up with the movement, almost as part of it, but, so far as my narrative is a personal one, it is only

so because we are still living in the midst of the events which
I shall describe. I cannot pretend to any impartiality in my
judgement either of men or of affairs, but I believe that the
prejudice or bias to which I have already pleaded guilty is
one which will increasingly display itself as an important
factor in the life of Scotland as a whole.

CHAPTER TWO

I BECAME INVOLVED in politics by accident, as the result
of an unpremeditated intervention in a University debate.
I had first matriculated in Glasgow University in 1923, and,
as a law student, I was under the necessity of serving an
apprenticeship in an office in the city while taking classes
first in Arts and then in Law. There was, therefore, very
little opportunity for taking part in the corporate life of the
University and for several years it never occurred to me to
do so. One evening, however, I was induced by a friend to
go up to the Union to hear a mock Parliamentary debate.
The debating hall in the old Union in Glasgow University,
which is now, alas, given over entirely to women students,
was modelled on the House of Commons, and Parliamentary
debates were carried on there on Friday evenings with all the
pomp and ceremony, and with probably greater eloquence
than in the Mother of Parliaments itself. There was on this
occasion more room on the Labour Opposition benches
than on the Government side and for this very practical
reason my friend and I found ourselves at least temporarily
among the supporters of the Labour Party.

During the period for open debate there was a sudden lull
in the proceedings. The Speaker of the House had twice
made it plain that anyone not on the Front Benches who
cared to rise would catch his eye but for the moment no one
accepted his invitation. My companion nudged me in the
ribs. "I'll bet you're scared to get up and speak," he muttered. Without a moment's premeditation, spurred by that
whispered challenge, I rose to my feet and found myself, to
my own intense surprise, declaiming in a firm and clear

voice, "Mr. Speaker, sir, you have given me three minutes in which to address the House. In these three minutes I shall endeavour to save Scotland and the Empire from the ruin which my friends across the floor have made all but inevitable. . . ." I cannot remember what followed, nor even what was the subject of debate, but these few words, the first I had ever uttered in public, remain as clearly printed in my memory as if they had been learned from some lesson or spoken by someone other than myself. For three long minutes I continued to harangue the house, astonished and not a little pleased at having discovered an entirely unsuspected fluency. My remarks were punctuated in proper style, both with laughter and applause, and when I sat down I knew that, for some extraordinary reason, I had made a hit with that highly critical student audience.

A few minutes later no less august a person than the Leader of the Opposition himself—the President of the University Labour Club—was at my side congratulating me and asking me to join the Labour Club Committee. I hesitated. "Look here," he said, "our Treasurer has just resigned and I'll get you nominated for the job. It's most important, and you'll be Secretary next term." Thus, lured by the sudden prospect of high office, I accepted, and I have been involved in politics ever since! From then onwards I was a regular Front Bench speaker at the Union debates and soon, indeed, was elevated to one of the most coveted positions in the student hierarchy—Convener of Debates.

At that time the Independent Labour Party was the active missionary force in Labour politics in Scotland and its organiser, Willie Stewart, and his assistant, James Carmichael, were always on the lookout for new speakers. A natural recruiting ground was the University Labour Club and, before long, I was enrolled as a member of the

Glasgow City Branch of the I.L.P. and was active as a propagandist all over Scotland and even in Northern Ireland and the North of England. Socialism in those days was not the doctrine of the State-planned economy which it has since become. The I.L.P. had inherited much of the old Radical tradition of Scotland and for the most part as a street-corner missionary I was expected not to expound the theories of Karl Marx but merely to give expression to the general sense of injustice and aspiration for a better way of life which were very natural feelings among the workers of Clydeside in the years between the wars. Although I had begun without any strong political convictions I found it easy to accommodate myself to I.L.P. propaganda and thoroughly enjoyed the almost religious atmosphere of enthusiasm in which we all worked.

For eighteen months I remained a member both of the University Labour Club and of the I.L.P. Looking back, I suppose I was well on the way to a political career, but of that I had no thought. I was still in my early twenties, and I was in it for the fun of the game as much as because I believed that there were many wrongs to be righted in the world. There was one item on the party programme, however, about which I soon became enthusiastic and around which I began to build most of my propaganda speeches—Home Rule for Scotland.

Ever since the days of Keir Hardie the I.L.P. was committed to support that proposal. Many of the Party's best-known speakers were professed believers in the need for a Scottish Parliament. Men like Tom Johnston, the late Rev. James Barr, James Maxton and many others, while they seldom gave Home Rule a foremost place in their thoughts were genuine in their attachment to the idea and even Ramsay MacDonald himself had in his early days been Secretary of a London Scottish Home Rule Association.

I think that most of them had a special sentimental compartment in their minds and it was there that they cherished as a somewhat distant dream the idea of Scotland governing herself. Many of them had begun their political life as Liberals in the Gladstonian tradition and Home Rule was inherited along with other items of the Radical faith. As the years went on and as positions of power and influence opened up to them, they gradually forgot their Scottish sentiment and like so many other Scotsmen of their time concentrated their energies in a Party loyalty which far transcended national considerations.

Perhaps because I suspected that some such tendency was already in evidence I began to feel uneasy in my membership of the Labour Party. The more I thought about things the more I became convinced that Scottish Home Rule was the one great reform which must be lifted above all party interests and was also the reform most likely to effect an immediate and tangible improvement in our Scottish conditions of life and to fill our people with a new morale. In the summer of 1927 I was sent to accompany John L. Kinloch who was at that time Labour candidate for Argyll, on a propaganda tour of the Island of Mull. Although I had been born in Glasgow my family came from Mull and Iona and because of my connections with these islands it was thought that I could be useful in breaking new ground for the Labour cause. For two weeks Kinloch and I went round the island addressing meetings in every *clachan*. He was as keen a Home Ruler as I was myself and nearly all our speeches were devoted to this topic. We found our audiences were far more sympathetic to it than they were to Socialism and our own conversations after meetings were increasingly turned upon the subject.

I was little more than a youth, new to politics and impatient to get things done. Kinloch was middle-aged, a teacher both by profession and by vocation, and he had been for years a leading speaker for the Labour Party in Scotland. But for his complete personal integrity and his ignorance of the art of wire-pulling he would by then have had a safe Labour seat in Parliament. Instead he was throwing himself wholeheartedly into the difficult task of pioneering for Socialism in the Highlands. Repeatedly I asked him the question uppermost in my mind, whether the Labour Party if it came to power would give priority to Scotland's claims. Though his natural Party loyalty as well as his loyalty to friends of a lifetime made him hesitate to say so I soon gathered that he had little real faith in the Party's eagerness to carry out its Scottish programme.

"Give it a chance," he would say. "If people like ourselves keep prodding from behind we can keep the Party up to its promises. Besides, there's no other way. The Tory Party is against it. The Liberal Party is out of the count. The Labour Party is the only Party of reform and we must work through it." But I was not satisfied, and by the time we returned to Glasgow I had made up my mind to leave the Labour Party and to do whatever I could to make Scottish Home Rule a live issue and an issue which would transcend the differences among Tories, Liberals or Socialists. No doubt I was evincing the audacity of youth. There were others in Scotland of like mind with myself but, at that time, I knew nothing about them and had never even heard of their activities. So far as I was then aware, at the age of twenty-two I was going to embark on the extraordinary adventure of creating a new movement and throwing out a challenge to the parties then entrenched in power. When I got home the first person to whom I confided my intentions was my mother. She had been a lifelong Liberal, a devotee like many other Highland people of Lloyd George, and she had always poured friendly scorn on my Labour Party activities. "Now she'll be pleased,"

I thought, "when I tell her that I'm going to resign." Unknown to me, however, she must have been cherishing secret ambitions of a political future for me. When I told her what I was going to do she bristled suddenly.

"Home Rule for Scotland, indeed!" she exclaimed. "That died at Culloden. You'll be daft if you throw your future to the winds chasing that old dream."

Then almost wistfully she added, "Home Rule—if only we could get it! What a great thing it would be for Scotland!"

CHAPTER THREE

My FIRST TASK on my return to University life was, of course, to obtain supporters for the cause. My two closest associates in the Labour Club were James Valentine, its Vice-President, and T. F. Rodger, Assistant Secretary, and with them I began a series of discussions which soon ended in their being converted to the idea of Home Rule. I found, indeed, when I talked to them that they also had felt the stirrings of national consciousness and that when the idea of a national movement was expounded to them they were more than open-minded about it.

One evening, late in September, 1927, as we sipped tea in a Sauchiehall Street café, the three of us boldly constituted ourselves as Glasgow University Scottish Nationalist Association. The minutes of the meeting were recorded on the back of an envelope by Fergus Rodger. We were half in fun, all in earnest.

I now have every reason to believe that Scotland will gain self-government in the near future. Any such change in the Constitution of the United Kingdom will have far-reaching effects in the whole British Commonwealth and in Europe as well. It is, therefore, not wholly absurd to say that the adventure then begun by three Glasgow students may have played its small part in reshaping the world!

Having formed our Association our next concern was to enrol a membership. Without much difficulty and with a complete lack of Party loyalty, we soon suborned a fair number of our ex-colleagues in the University Labour Party and felt ourselves justified in calling a public meeting in the Union.

The meeting was highly successful. The Debating Hall was crowded and, although few of those present took the new idea very seriously it became obvious at Question Time that most of them were at least prepared to think about it.

There was, of course, the usual amount of student barracking. One heckler wanted to know if Scotland would have her own king and would I then become King John? Thus was born a nickname which, for better or for worse, has followed me ever since. Somebody else suggested that an immediate raiding party should be formed so that the Stone of Destiny might be recovered from Westminster for the Coronation ceremony. It was all conducted in the best of good spirits and, at the end of the day, we enrolled over fifty members. The new members, of course, immediately adjourned to the Committee Room to celebrate in the usual student fashion and our hilarity proved sufficiently infectious to double our numbers before the party came unsteadily to an end.

Thereafter, the newly formed Association went from strength to strength. Soon we were participating in our own right in Parliamentary debates, and, since we had no parent party outside the University, we could say exactly what we liked and invent a new policy for every occasion. This proved such an attraction to men of independent mind that, before long, we could include in our membership nearly all the brightest spirits of that University generation.

I have our first membership card before me as I write. Our object was stated to be:

"To foster and maintain Scottish Nationalism by (1) securing self-government for Scotland and (2) advancing the ideals of Scottish culture within and without the University."

It will be seen from that bold proclamation that we did not intend to confine our efforts to Gilmorehill and soon we were enquiring whether there were not others like us in Scotland. The first we discovered was Roland Eugene Muirhead, General Secretary of the Scottish Home Rule Association. Neither I nor any of my colleagues had been aware of the existence of such an organisation. But, after a report of one of our meetings in the Union had appeared in the Press, we received a letter from Mr. Muirhead on headed notepaper asking us to get in touch with him. I well remember Jim Valentine's comment when he opened the letter.

"This solves the problem," he exclaimed. "We'll get a donation for our funds from the Home Rule Association!"

The problem being, of course, that, like most University organisations, we were already in debt and unlike the Tory, Liberal or Labour Clubs we had no grandmotherly central office to which to apply when in difficulties.

Valentine was immediately delegated to interview Muirhead with instructions to seek a contribution of not less than £100. He came back empty-handed! Mr. Muirhead, it seemed, was an elderly man, slow of speech and faintly distrustful of any student activity. The Home Rule Association itself had no funds and its office in Elmbank Crescent was dingy and unimpressive. Altogether, the report from our plenipotentiary was highly discouraging, except for one item of news. Apparently the Home Rule Association was in the act of bringing together, for the second or third time, a meeting under the title of a National Convention which would be attended by representatives of various trade unions, a few local authorities and one or two other Home Rule organisations. This Convention would be an important event. A Home Rule Bill, approved by a previous Convention, had been brought up in Parliament by the Rev. James Barr, M.P., and Thomas Johnston, M.P., but had been talked out. The new Convention would, therefore, discuss what further steps must be tâken to advance the cause.

We, of course, were invited to send delegates to the Convention and, in due course, Valentine and myself presented ourselves there. The meeting took place in the Highlanders Institute in Glasgow. It was attended by about 100 delegates, mostly from trade union branches and by half a dozen Labour M.Ps. headed by the Rev. James Barr. An organisation known as the Scottish National Movement was represented by the poet and journalist Lewis Spence, supported by Miss Wendy Wood. Another organisation, apparently of a more extreme character, called the Scots National League, was not officially represented but made its presence heard if not felt by angry interruptions from the public gallery.

The proceedings were, to say the least, inconclusive. No one seemed to know quite why the meeting was being held. Lewis Spence suggested that a National Party should now be formed, and James Barr immediately pointed out that no Labour Party member could be associated with any such proposal. The debate wandered backwards and forwards and finally petered out without any real decision of any kind being made.

Valentine and I came away with heavy hearts. We had gone to this Convention full of high hopes that at last we might find a body outside the University with which we could co-operate. We became convinced instead that, if any such body was to come into being, we should have to call it into existence ourselves. We were young, we were inexperienced, we were penniless, and we hadn't the slightest idea how to begin.

CHAPTER FOUR

WITHIN A FEW weeks of the 1927 Convention the Committee of the University Nationalist Association resolved to call a meeting representative of all Home Rule organisations and to put before them the proposition that a National Party should be formed. From that decision there stemmed a series of conferences among delegates from the Scots National League, the Scottish National Movement, the Scottish Home Rule Association and the University Association which finally, in April, 1928, resulted in agreement to merge and thus to form the National Party of Scotland.

I cannot say that agreement was easy to reach. All the infinite capacity of the Scots to bicker over definitions, words and even commas was fully displayed throughout the period of negotiation. Often Valentine and I, who represented the University, and who acted in the negotiating committee as Secretary and Chairman respectively, were either privately amused or thoroughly exasperated by the endless arguments which took place. To us it did not seem to matter very much how our objectives were stated as long as we could create an organisation aiming by and large at a measure of Home Rule, but to our seniors it seemed as though we were actually framing a whole Constitution for a new Scotland.

I remember, for example, the heated discussions which took place as to how our objects could be stated so as to satisfy those who wished to break away completely from England and the others who had slightly milder views. At last a compromise was devised and the object of the National Party was proclaimed: "To secure self-government for Scotland with independent national status within the British group of nations." Even the word "Commonwealth" was thus expunged from our vocabulary!

Argument, of course, was inevitable, for we were a very mixed crowd. The Scots National League had been formed under the inspiration of the late William Gillies and the late Angus Clark, two Highlanders exiled, and reasonably prosperous in London. They were advocates of complete separation and their monthly journal, the *Scots Independent*, regularly spat contempt on everything English. They were ably represented at all the joint meetings by Tom Gibson, a fiery red-headed lawyer's clerk who later became Secretary of the British Steel Federation in London and, now back in Scotland, is President of the Scottish National Party.

He combined an almost unparalleled wealth of knowledge about industrial Scotland with a capacity to get so enthusiastic in argument that he almost literally drowned all opposition. With a pen he could express himself in precise and incisive terms, but in speech he was apt to triplicate every remark. He regarded it as his task to ensure that the National Party which might emerge from our talks would be an incorruptible enemy of all English political parties.

Completely different in temperament and outlook was Lewis Spence, President of the Scottish National Movement and one of the most brilliant poets of the Scottish renaissance. Despite his poetry, however, he looked and usually acted like a cautious writer to the signet. He habitually wore spats and a bowler hat, which, to my youthful mind, detracted greatly from his literary reputation. He was an enthusiast for Scotland but had no great interest in politics and often exasperated Gibson by his somewhat woolly ideas about them. His team-mate of those days was an extremely short-sighted Edinburgh lawyer who wore a red-gold wig and who was known, if not in the minutes of the proceedings, at least to Valentine and myself as Goldilocks. He was in fact a generous and kindly man, and though he seldom spoke, when he did it was usually to pour oil on troubled waters and often to find the kind of verbal compromise which lawyers love.

The central figure of those meetings, however, was Roland Muirhead representing the Home Rule Association which he had carried on his own shoulders for a good many years. I have never known anyone more single-minded in the pursuit of an objective than he. He was as difficult to negotiate with as granite is to carve, but, whenever the combined arguments of his colleagues at last pushed him into a new position, he would entrench himself there as immovably as in his former redoubt. He was of the calibre of the old Covenanters who defied the Government's dragoons and gladly died for their faith. Like them he made up in sincerity what he lacked in humour and, although he was a wealthy man, he always dressed shabbily in a kind of hodden grey well suited for a conventicle on the moor. He must now be over his eightieth year but he is still plodding on, in a furrow of his own, with the goal of a free Scotland before him. I have seldom agreed with him either in his notions of political strategy or in the intransigence of his views but there are few men for whom I have had a greater admiration and respect. Many of the finest qualities of the Lowland Scot are exemplified in him.

Such were the people who founded the National Party of Scotland. Looking back, and knowing how sincerely each held his own point of view I think it is a tribute to their genuine concern for Scotland that they managed even for a few years to sink their differences and work together for their cause.

The National Party thus conceived was destined to a stormy career and to many schisms. But there can be no doubt that it and its successors have already played a vital part in the history of Scotland and have in not much more than twenty years, completely changed the mental and spiritual atmosphere in which our people live. Between the two great wars no nation suffered from industrial depression as did Scotland. Something like 600,000 of her small population emigrated and the despair which drove them forth was reflected among those who stayed at home by a kind of angry apathy. The enterprise and ingenuity with which the Scots of the nineteenth century had made their little country the most prosperous in the world seemed to have disappeared. In their place had arisen a sterile class rancour wholly alien to the tradition of Scotland but which was the inevitable outcome of grinding poverty, iniquitous housing conditions and the hopelessness of mass unemployment. The selfish complacency of the better-off and the envy of the less fortunate became the touchstones of political difference. They are a poor substitute for that deep-seated sense of community which historically has always knit the people of this country together in times of adversity. The formation of the National Party by a handful of enthusiasts whom their countrymen regarded as cranks was at that dark time a new declaration of faith in the community of Scotland.

It was a declaration, however, which at first very few people heard. The daily Press paid scant attention to us and although we scraped together enough money to hire a three-roomed suite of offices in West Regent Street in Glasgow, we had little idea how to compel the world to hear our message.

Yet, quite suddenly, by a stroke of luck, our fortunes changed and Scottish nationalism reached the headlines.

CHAPTER FIVE

STUDENTS OF THE Scottish universities have the privilege every three years of electing their Lord Rector who is Chairman of the University Court, and, therefore, titular head of the University. In Glasgow an election fell due in October, 1928, and it had always been the custom there for the political clubs to make the occasion one for a display of party fervour. For many years the Tory Party had maintained a monopoly of the office and now they announced that their candidate would be Stanley Baldwin, then at the height of his fame as Prime Minister.

The Liberals nominated Sir Herbert Samuel (now Lord Samuel) and the Socialists Mr. Rosslyn Mitchell, at that time Member of Parliament for Paisley. We Nationalists were in a quandary. Obviously here was an opportunity to call attention to our case but we had neither money nor a candidate. Our difficulty was to think of anyone of sufficient standing to aspire to the high office of Lord Rector, who would at the same time endorse the objects of the Nationalist Association. At first, the only person we could think of was Sir James Barrie, who had recently made a big hit as a non-political Rector in St. Andrews. Valentine, as Secretary of the Association, composed a letter to him which I thought was a masterpiece of diplomacy. It suggested that our aims were not really political and that we desired to break the dominance of the political parties in Glasgow Rectorial elections. But the answer was a brief refusal!

It was then that the name of R. B. Cunninghame Graham came vaguely into my mind, but when I mentioned him to my student colleagues they all confessed that they knew nothing about him and, therefore, turned down the choice. I was not satisfied and in the evening when I should have been studying for an exam in the Mitchell Library I took out, instead of textbooks, one of Cunninghame Graham's volumes of essays called *Hope*.

As I read I became fascinated both by the man and his writing. Here was a really great Scotsman and, although his name was unfamiliar to my own generation, I was sure we could soon remedy that. But what were his politics? I knew that in his very young days he had been a Radical and had later taken part with Keir Hardie in the formation of the Labour Party. But, for many years, he had been missing from the political scene altogether and, indeed, seemed to have spent most of his time, as Don Roberto, in South America.

By this time, however, I was so eager that I turned to my neighbour at the Library desk and asked him if he knew anything about Cunninghame Graham. "Yes," he said, "isn't he the chap whom Bernard Shaw wrote up in *Captain Brassbound's Conversion*?"

In a few minutes I was reading the Preface to that play, and, if I had any doubts about the suitability of Graham as a candidate, Bernard Shaw dispelled them!

It didn't take long to convince the University Committee that he should be approached and this time we did not try any diplomacy. We wrote to Cunninghame Graham, told him about our Nationalist Association and the part it had played in founding the National Party and asked him to accept nomination as a Nationalist candidate. We omitted to tell him that our funds amounted to about 3*s.*, but that was a matter which we thought could look after itself later on.

Within three or four days we received a reply. It was slightly noncommittal, but encouraging. Obviously he was not scared of being called a Nationalist but he wanted to be assured that our approach to him was genuine and not a mere student hoax. He was to be in Glasgow in a week's time and would be pleased to see one or two of us in the Central Hotel, when he would give us his yea or nay.

After some deliberation we appointed Valentine as our ambassador and left everything to his powers of persuasion.

Valentine reported to me in the Union where I waited impatiently after his interview. "Well," he said, "we've got a candidate—and I think he's the greatest Scotsman alive!"

Eagerly I questioned him about Cunninghame Graham, whom I had never seen except in my own mind's eye. He described him with such enthusiasm that soon we were discussing chances of victory in the election—though our Association was not yet a year old and was puny in numbers compared with any of the established political clubs.

When the time came to announce our candidate's name at an open meeting in the Union (the tradition being that it should be held secret till then) we could find no suitable sponsoring speaker from outside and I, therefore, undertook the task myself. The debating hall was in its usual state of uproar and hundreds of copies of a leaflet were floating from the gallery. I picked one up from the platform floor and glanced at it before I began to speak. It was headed "Monsieur Faute de Barrie" followed by an unflattering caricature of Cunninghame Graham and a few lines of questionable French verse. Someone in our midst had betrayed our secret to the Labour Club and they had made good use of their knowledge by keeping it till the last moment and then completely taking the wind out of my sails. My speech was a flop![1]

In spite of that bad beginning I think it is true to say that in October, 1928, we ran one of the greatest Rectorial

[1]The author of that pungent leaflet was Roger McDougall, now a distinguished London playwright.

campaigns ever known in Glasgow University. Since we could not rely on any well-known public figures as speakers we did nearly all the speaking ourselves. At first we were scorned as rank outsiders but gradually we began to command a hearing. It was of great advantage to us that the distinguished politicians who visited the Union to speak for our opponents knew very little about University affairs and were wholly ignorant about the office of Lord Rector. Early in the campaign I discovered that they could all be completely stumped by a very simple question, asked on a point of order halfway through the first sentence of their speech: "Mr. Chairman, has the speaker any right to address this audience unless he can tell us what are the duties of Lord Rector in a Scottish University?" The ensuing uproar increasingly became one united shout from the audience— "Answer the question! Answer the question!" which, apart altogether from the noise, the poor speaker could seldom do.

The first major success from these tactics occurred when Sir John Gilmour as Secretary of State for Scotland, was to speak on behalf of Baldwin. The usual question was asked and when Sir John floundered for an answer there was a sudden shout, not altogether unpremeditated on our part, from a crowd in the gallery above the platform—"Get off Sir John and give King John a chance to tell you the answer". Sir John, not unnaturally, became angry and flustered, which was fatal to his cause. In a moment he was swept by a surging crowd into the wings and at the same instant I was hoisted by a dozen shoulders on to the platform and commanded to make a speech.

From that time we did not suffer much from our lack of funds. Instead of incurring the expense of meetings of our own we coolly commandeered the platform of all our opponents and ultimately by various devices took over their social functions as well. That kind of audacity is, of course, dear to the heart of Scottish students and soon we were inundated by new recruits pressing their 6*d*. membership fee upon us.

The final result of it all was no less astonishing to ourselves than to our opponents. When the poll was counted on 27th October, 1928, Stanley Baldwin crept in by a meagre majority of sixty votes over Cunninghame Graham. The other candidates were nowhere in the running and what made matters even worse for the Tories was that we had a clear majority of men students in all four "nations". It was the "flappers", to whom Baldwin had recently granted the parliamentary franchise, who had tilted the scales in his favour and thereafter we dubbed him the first Lady Rector.

It had been taken so much for granted that Baldwin would be elected by the usual sweeping Tory majority that the Scottish Press had given very little notice to the campaign and practically none to the strange new phenomenon of a Nationalist candidate who was certain to collect only a handful of votes. The actual result, however, was so astounding that immediately the problem of Scottish Home Rule leapt into the headlines. Even the sober-minded and hostile *Glasgow Herald* opened its columns for two weeks to a lengthy discussion by prominent contributors stating both sides of the case.

Both at the University and in our National Party offices in West Regent Street hundreds of letters arrived from all over Scotland, and far further afield, seeking information and offering help. The party which had been born so quietly a few months before was now a real factor in the life of Scotland.

CHAPTER SIX

During the Rectorial campaign two people of great distinction had intimated their support for our candidate. One was the Duke of Montrose, descendant of the great Marquess who had left so vivid a mark on the pages of Scotland's history, and the other was Compton Mackenzie who, although he had been born and bred in England was proud of his Scottish blood.

I have rarely seen anybody so elated by anything as was Compton Mackenzie by the declaration of our result. He had waited for it along with Cunninghame Graham himself, in an Edinburgh hotel, and within a couple of hours I had a telegram from him expressing something of his enthusiasm.

I had met him for the first time a few days before when he had come, quite off his own bat, from London to Glasgow to see whether he could help us. Of course, I thought then, and still do, that he was one of the most fascinating men I had ever come across. He was clean-shaven in those days and an unfortunate morning accident had knocked out two teeth in his upper denture. When he smiled this made him look as harmlessly sinister as Captain Hook. His conversation bubbled forth and his eagerness about our campaign was obvious. We arranged for him to come up to a meeting in the Union to speak on Cunninghame Graham's behalf, and, although I believe it was the first time he had ever spoken politically in public, he was a great success. Unlike many distinguished people he tolerated student barracking with so friendly a manner that he soon commanded a silent audience. I think the impression which he then made

contributed in no small degree to his success as Nationalist
candidate for the Rectorship three years later.

Since we now had a few people of public standing to
speak for us, we immediately arranged to hold a public
meeting in St. Andrews Hall in Glasgow with Cunninghame
Graham at the top of the bill and the Duke of Montrose and
Compton Mackenzie to support him. Although we had only
a few days to advertise it, it was a great success and the hall
was packed by an audience of nearly 3,000, including a
large number of students who almost raised the roof with
boisterous applause when Cunninghame Graham rose to
speak.

No one, of course, had a more magnificent presence than
he. He was tall and lithe and his moustache and beard
served to accentuate the aristocratic line of his features. His
oratory was of Victorian vintage but he was a master of the
art. Every studied gesture added to the force of his words
and though his periods were often long they never became
involved. Even in his old age he had a voice which was
clear and strong and could be heard in every corner of the
hall without the help of loud-speaking equipment, which he
heartily despised and would always wave away with an
imperious lift of hand and arm.

His speech that night was a great declaration of faith in
the future of Scotland and an affirmation of his own personal
dedication to the cause of self-government. Thereafter, by
unanimous consent, he was made President of the National
Party and until his death in 1936 he was always at our service
for every big meeting. I came to know him extremely well
and the more I saw of him the more deeply I admired him.
He possessed all the finest qualities of a Scottish aristocrat,
made all the more vivid by the air of a *hidalgo* which he had
inherited from a Spanish ancestress.

I think he was out of sympathy with the times in which he

lived. As a young man a brilliant political career was opening up for him but he threw up his seat in Parliament and became one of the leaders of the working-class movement, having even been arrested for his part in leading a dockers' procession during a strike in London. Although he would have called himself a Socialist in those days, he was the most completely individualistic man I have ever known. His brilliant writings followed no set fashion. They were neither essays nor short stories but were like the distilled quintessence of the conversation of a delightful mind. Early in life the impoverishment of his family had compelled him to sell the ancestral home at Gartmore near Aberfoyle, and I think he always felt foot-loose after that break with the past. His love of his own country, and of his own countryside, was well expressed by himself when he said, in his *History of the District of Menteith*:

"The Isle of Rest still seems to float upon the lake. In the green sedges wild ducks settle with a whirr of wings, and in the shallows pike lie basking in the sun. The hills still are reflected in the frosted, silver mirror of the lake, as in a mirage. The monks who built the long, grey church, sleep all forgotten, unconscious that they wove the spell, that still enchants, the island and the lake. Better that they sleep on, for who could wish for any better resting place, lulled by the lapping waves, and the soft murmur of the wind against the bulrushes. Perhaps, who knows, for everything is possible to natural science, and to faith, they do awake at times, and forming in procession, file into the chancel of their ruined church. As they pause for a moment before entering the choir, their ghostly abbot well may hear, what seems to him, the slogan of the wild MacGregors, coming down the hill. He need not shudder, or prepare to signal to the Earl's

Castle on the Isle of Talla, to wake his men at arms, for
what he hears will only be a motor horn, and he can pray
his fill."

He was the true type of the wandering Scot, soldier of
fortune and philosopher combined, and though he died in
distant South America, by his own wish his body was
brought home to be buried on Inchmahome on his beloved
Lake of Menteith. The coffin was carried into the little
church of Port of Menteith, draped in the sombre tartan of
the Grahams, and there his many friends and all the country-
folk from round about took farewell of him. Then with a
piper in the prow playing "The Flowers of the Forest" his
body was rowed across the loch to the island where Mary of
Scotland had spent the happiest days of her childhood. The
wanderer, who had travelled so far and in so many strange
places where no white man had ever been before, had at last
returned home.

He was a king among men, descendant of the Earls of
Menteith who boasted that their blood was redder than the
King's. In all likelihood he was the senior living representative of Scotland's royal line of Stewarts, of Robert Bruce
and of Kenneth MacAlpin who was crowned in 843. But he
had no lust for power and to him there were neither his
superiors nor his inferiors but only his fellow men.

The Duke of Montrose, who joined Cunninghame
Graham on the platform that night, was also a Graham and
the head of the family. Though he was handicapped by
nearly complete deafness, he distinguished himself throughout many years by the part he played in the public life of
Scotland. He was of quite a different stamp from his
kinsman. Cunninghame Graham was in politics (and in the
best sense of the word) an adventurer who took keen
delight in crossing swords with the Party Goliaths and who

gave little thought to any of the practical considerations which might weigh with other men. The Duke, on the other hand, was fully conscious of his responsibilities as a leader of opinion and was able very shrewdly to assess the worth and the political chances of the new movement.

Although he declared himself to be wholly in favour of a measure of Scottish Home Rule he set his face completely against anything in the nature of separation from England and he declined our invitation to join the National Party. He heartily disliked the fringe of "wild men" who were already becoming vocal on our flanks and they in characteristic manner returned his dislike with every kind of accusation of betrayal. In later years he was to become my close colleague and I learned to value his advice and absolutely to trust his sincere and unselfish patriotism. But in the enthusiasm of youth I felt that night that he was altogether too canny and thought we could get along well enough without him.

I think one of the people who alarmed him was C. M. Grieve who as Hugh McDiarmid is now widely recognised as one of Scotland's greatest poets. Grieve had joined our platform and in characteristic manner had hurled contempt at everything English. Although I have no doubt that he has done invaluable work in the whole field of Scottish literature I am certain that C. M. Grieve has been politically one of the greatest handicaps with which any national movement could have been burdened. His love of bitter controversy, his extravagant and self-assertive criticism of the English, and his woolly thinking, which could encompass within one mind the doctrines both of Major Douglas and Karl Marx, were taken by many of the more sober-minded of the Scots as sufficient excuse to condemn the whole case for Home Rule out of hand.

These were the people who made the first big public

appearance for the National Party. All the speeches were well reported even including my own, and there followed much correspondence in all the Scottish daily Press. I remember one anonymous letter which, pouring contempt on the whole occasion, described our platform as having been occupied by one Duke, one Spanish nobleman, one English novelist, one poet and one Irish tenor! Thus was I confused with the great!

CHAPTER SEVEN

It seemed, by November, 1928, that we were riding high on the crest of an irresistible wave. Our honorary organising secretary was one Henry Balderstone, an ex-sergeant-major of the Guards and now a minor civil servant, who sent all those of us who could string a few words together to meetings all over Scotland. We went at his command with all the enthusiasm of men who knew they were right and on the winning side. Public interest was at a high level and everywhere we were received by large and boisterous audiences. Branches of the National Party sprang up almost spontaneously all over Scotland and funds, albeit small, began to accumulate in our coffers.

Then, in December of that year, by the chance of death or promotion, a Parliamentary by-election fell due in the constituency of North Midlothian. Although most of us were flushed by the heady wine of success the challenge which a by-election presented made us pause. We had boasted, on the strength of our University success, that we would challenge the political parties in every contest but we had scarcely reckoned with the possibility of a trial of strength so soon.

A meeting of our National Council was hastily summoned to consider the emergency. With almost one voice some fifty of us round the table counselled caution. We had little money, less experience and no likely candidate in view. But the unanimity of hesitance was suddenly broken by Lewis Spence.

"I'm tired of all this pusillanimity," he declared. "If no one else will do it I'll fight this by-election myself."

No statement could have been more surprising to us all. Lewis Spence was the least belligerent of men and not one of us would have pictured him in the role of martyr warrior. Yet, there he was, so filled with faith in the cause, and so rightly dismayed by our cold calculation of the cost, that we were almost tongue-tied before his challenge. After a few half-hearted protests the die was cast and we were committed to nominate him as our candidate.

Our announcement to the Press caused a considerable stir. No one knew our real strength and, after all, we had already brought off a near-success in Glasgow University. Ponderous leading articles were written in the daily newspapers counselling the electors to look twice at this strange new phenomenon. The political parties began to vie with each other in vague promises to do something about Scotland. Hundreds of new recruits rolled up to our offices to offer their help and even occasionally to subscribe to our funds.

Meantime, of course, we were ourselves in a state of near panic. Not one of us had ever taken part in a Parliamentary election and we had nothing but the vaguest ideas of organisation or even of all the legal preliminaries of nominating a candidate. Since I was a law student I was deputed to study the Franchise Acts and to advise the Council on all the steps which must be taken. A self-styled professional organiser was wished upon us by our London Branch and was engaged at a salary far beyond our means to pay. Committee rooms were taken in Dalkeith, the centre of the constituency, halls were booked for meetings and with a minimum of amateurish prearrangement we launched forth into our campaign.

At first we commanded a good public and an interested if not friendly Press. Rapidly, however, the goodwill which greeted us in the beginning dwindled away. Our organiser proved to be a highly excitable little man who knew nothing whatever about high-pressure political campaigning. One of his favourite faults was to summon a battery of untrained speakers from Glasgow to a meeting at X and when they arrived there they would find that the only meeting arranged for that night was at Y, some ten miles away. Naturally, the friendly public grew tired of waiting for meetings which never transpired and when, finally, we overcame our teething troubles it was difficult to gather any audience at all.

Nor was our candidate the right man for the job. Lewis Spence is one of the most lovable of men, but he is no politician. Time and again he answered questions so clumsily as to give our opponents handfuls of ammunition to fire against us. He was even once so misguided as to report to the Press that someone with sinister intent had fired a pistol at him as he journeyed from one meeting to another, but investigation revealed that the culprit had been a schoolboy with a toy repeater. At the biggest rally we had organised, on the eve of poll, he rose to address an audience which was willing to be enthused, recalled that had it not been for the by-election he would that night have been addressing a Burns Supper, and proceeded to give his Burns oration. To make matters worse, the oration was in verse, couched in Middle Scots, and was very long indeed. It was magnificent, but it was not politics.

The result was inevitable. When the votes were counted we learned that we had received some 830 out of a poll of close on 40,000! Well do I remember the delighted comments of the hostile Press. One newspaper went so far as to say that nothing more would ever be heard of Scottish nationalism and proceeded to perform unflattering obsequies over our remains.

To all of us who had taken part in the campaign, it was, of course, a bitter disappointment though the edge was taken off it in so far as we had gradually learned to expect it. We realised that we had made a cardinal mistake in plunging so soon and so ill-prepared into an election, and we knew that we had lost for ever the first impetus which might with more care have pushed us far on the road to success.

Such little funds as we had were completely dissipated and for years thereafter our Party struggled along from hand to mouth carrying an increasing burden of debt. On the credit side, however, we had gained something in experience and had begun to build up a team of effective propagandists, many of whom had never spoken on a platform before. For my own part, it was during those weeks of campaigning that I made some lifelong friendships among my fellow speakers. There were J. M. McNicol, who had been a leading figure in the University a year or two before my time; A. M. Gray and his brother Bertie (who is now Vice-Chairman of the Covenant Association), R. R. MacEwen of Inverness whose father, Sir Alexander MacEwen, Provost of Inverness, was later to play a leading part in our movement, and a number of others. We were all young, and although we were politically inexperienced, it is not unfair to claim that we made a speaking team which the big political parties could not rival. With additions to our numbers from time to time, we campaigned in every corner of Scotland and at many a future election we could command packed halls when our opponents were speaking to empty benches.

Part of our secret was that although we were very serious about our cause we had no political ambitions and did not therefore need to take ourselves too seriously. Every campaign was to us a gay affair and wherever we went we were sure to find some *howff* where after meetings we could *ceilidh* till the small hours.

Looking back, I know very well that any one of these men with whom, from that time, I have been associated could easily have made for himself a political career in one of the major parties. Yet they preferred to remain comparatively unknown and to spend all their spare time and much of their spare cash in what they believed was their country's cause. They are all still deeply attached to the movement and no disappointment, no postponement of the hope of victory, has ever made them waver for one moment in their loyalty. However little their names may be known just now, they will some day rank high among the men who have made the new Scotland.

North Midlothian was, of course, only the beginning of a long series of elections in which we took part. I had already been nominated by the Eastern Glasgow Branch of the Party as prospective candidate for the Camlachie Division of Glasgow and shortly afterwards R. E. Muirhead was nominated for East Renfrewshire. In accepting these nominations we believed that we had plenty of time for preparation for there seemed to be no early likelihood of a General Election. Unfortunately for us, Baldwin decided to go to the country in June, 1929, and, before we had time to recover from North Midlothian, we found ourselves again in the throes of electioneering.

Once again our efforts were amateurish in the extreme. In Camlachie we hired committee rooms which were supplied with neither gas nor electricity and after dark all the multifarious work of addressing envelopes, packing election addresses and preparing canvass cards was done laboriously by volunteers in candlelight. Even Cunninghame Graham himself sat down at a table one night after a meeting and addressed envelopes for an hour or two in extremely illegible writing. Thereafter, he demonstrated feats of strength with a couple of heavy dining-room chairs which, to his great delight, none of us youngsters could emulate.

The candidate himself was kept busy night and day. Apart from speaking at six or seven meetings, mostly in the open air, I had to take my share of envelope writing and since I was the only one among us who was expert on the pavement with pipe-clay I also had to go out in the small hours to advertise the following day's meetings. I pride myself that they were as well publicised as any meetings held by my opponents!

My friend Bertie Gray often recounts his first experience of chairmanship at an election meeting. It was in the Black-friars Hall in Dennistoun and he had carefully prepared Chairman's remarks calculated to last five minutes including stops for laughter and applause. The meeting began at 7.30 p.m., and, according to his time-table, I was due to arrive from another meeting at 8 p.m. He, meantime, had the support of one other speaker, a student hastily impressed for a job which he had never done before, and between them both they were to keep the audience going till my arrival.

Unfortunately, the speech which he had estimated to last for five minutes took only two minutes to deliver. The supporting speaker whom he introduced as a well-known orator, came to an abrupt halt at the end of seven minutes. The Chairman was in a quandary. He was still new enough at the game to be without the usual time-filling chatter which bores so many audiences. But suddenly he had an inspiration. "Ladies and Gentleman," he said, "it would now be appropriate to take a collection. I appeal to you to support our Nationalist candidate to the utmost of your means." In a moment a couple of hats were being handed round, and the friendly chink of money in them was sweet music to the Chairman's ears. Everything, however, comes to an end and within five minutes the hats had gone round the whole hall. There was still no sign of the candidate and Bertie, for an instant nonplussed, wondered what to do. He was afraid to ask for questions lest neither he nor the speaker should be able to answer them. After what seemed to him to be an interminable pause, he made up his mind. He rose and delivered his introductory speech all over again in the same words and with the same pauses as before. Then he called on his well-known orator who likewise repeated. his performance, in precisely the same time. There being still no sign of the candidate he had then perforce to appeal for another collection. The audience responded with a good will and four times the whole performance was repeated.

Meantime, I was hastening as best I could from one end of the constituency to the other on a bicycle, which was the only means of conveyance I could afford. I would have kept to the timetable and saved the Blackfriars audience three collections, had it not been that my bicycle chain came off the driving wheel halfway on my journey. In desperation, lacking even a tram fare, I cast my bike aside and set out running up Bellgrove to the Hall. Naturally, I arrived both grimy and winded, and as I puffed on to the platform I whispered to the Chairman, now about to commence his fifth introductory speech, "Keep it going for a few minutes till I get my breath back!"

This was completely beyond him and immediately he called on me to address the audience. Fortunately, his good humour had put them in the proper mood and the meeting ended as a huge success. It is actually a fact that the final collection was even bigger than the first!

Such were the experiences through which we had to go before we became well-trained campaigners. In spite of them, we succeeded in Camlachie in doubling the North Midlothian vote, and the result in East Renfrew recorded a similar advance. My election expenses in Camlachie, apart from the lost deposit, amounted to only £80 and every penny of that sum was collected from audiences at meetings who, if they did not finally vote for us, at least turned up in ever increasing numbers to display their sympathy with our cause.

CHAPTER EIGHT

DURING THE NEXT three years the National Party made considerable if unspectacular progress. Candidates were put forward in successive by-elections in 1930 and 1931 in Shettleston (J. M. McNicol), East Renfrewshire (W. O. Brown) and St. Rollox (Elma Campbell), and in each we made steady progress, increasing our percentage of the poll each time and in the two latter cases saving the deposit by a comfortable margin. It became evident that what had been scoffed at as an ephemeral sport in the political life of Scotland was likely to endure and could outlive and draw strength from every defeat.

Our organisation throughout the country was also expanding. Although in most places it was difficult to attract more than a handful of people to our first meetings we usually succeeded in gaining a sufficient nucleus of enthusiastic recruits to establish a committee which would ultimately grow into an organised branch of the Party. Typical of our campaigning in those early days was a meeting which I held in Inverness in the autumn of 1929. Lacking any contact there, I had by correspondence booked the Town Hall and arranged for advertisements in the local Press. I took with me to act as Chairman one of our National Council members, a Mr. Hugh Paterson, who, because he was a Gaelic speaker, seemed to be a suitable Chairman at our first meeting in the Capital of the Highlands.

When we arrived on the platform of the Town Hall we had certainly no reason to be thrilled by our reception. A total audience of twenty-six people was scattered sparsely through a hall with a seating capacity of 400 or 500.

Probably because they were so widely separated from each other the members of the audience did not even mildly clap their hands but simply sat staring stonily at us. It was a difficult atmosphere in which to open what we had grandiosely described in our advertisements as the beginning of a great Highland campaign.

Nevertheless, the audience sat patiently through the Chairman's remarks and my own speech and even asked a question or two at the end. Finally, I appealed to any who were willing to discuss the formation of a branch to wait behind and, to my surprise, four people actually did so. One of them was a young solicitor, Mr. Duncan H. McNeill, and another was Neil M. Gunn, then an Excise officer who had one novel to his credit and who quite soon afterwards leapt into fame by the publication of *Morning Tide*, one of the finest firstfruits of the new stirrings of Scottish consciousness in all the arts. Both of them were to become my life-long friends and to play a leading part in the national movement, but then only after some hesitation did they agree to see what they could do about setting up a small committee in Inverness. Within a few months they were able to report the establishment of a branch with over 500 members and money in the bank!

Another meeting was then arranged in the Town Hall, to be addressed by Compton Mackenzie and myself, and this time we had a full house and an enthusiastic welcome. From that time Inverness became one of the most active centres of Nationalism and meetings were planned from there all over the north, from Wick to Kyle and Kyle to Peterhead.

I loved those Highland campaigns and the new companionship which developed from them. Neil Gunn's house in Inverness, Larachan it was called, became our unofficial headquarters and no matter how late our return from distant parts we would find him waiting for us, eager for our report and ready to sit up talking with us till all hours. As an Exciseman he was precluded from speaking at our meetings, and, in any case, his own preference was to avoid the limelight, but, behind the scenes, he inspired us with his clear vision of the Scotland that should be.

Our talks ranged over the whole field of Nationalism and far beyond. We used to remark that as soon as the clock struck four in the morning we would find ourselves discussing the most abstract problems of the human soul and its relationship to God. Whether these discussions on that high plane ever reached any very definite conclusion is doubtful but there is no doubt that we began to formulate the ideas which have to a very large extent guided the development of the national movement in Scotland and, as I believe, made it something quite distinct and different from any parallel movement in other submerged European nations.

We had no feeling of hatred or even of dislike for things English nor did we labour under any deep sense of grievance or injustice. There had been plenty of black patches in the story of the relationship between the two countries even in the centuries since the Union but these were never the theme of our conversations. On the other hand, we believed that the history and racial origin of the two nations were so different that, in spite of their obvious relationship, each could make a very different contribution to the common pool of ideas, and each, if left to itself, would tend to approach similar problems in very dissimilar ways. It seemed obvious to us, therefore, that the submersion of Scotland in an incorporating Union with England was not only bad for Scotland but was also detrimental to the well-being of the whole island and of Europe too. It was as though what should have been a quartet in the concert of nations had degenerated into a one-man band.

In the light of that basic idea we discussed the history of our country and the whole course of its political and economic development. It is a remarkable fact that Scotland has had a longer continuous record as an independent and unconquered nation than any other country in Europe. In nearly two thousand years no conqueror has ever brought in his train a new and alien ruling class to subjugate the common people. Even the Norman adventurers to whom so many grants of land were made by David *I* came not as conquerors but as younger sons seeking the hands in marriage of the daughters of the native nobility. Robert Bruce himself, who is so often spoken of as an Anglo-Norman who more or less usurped the Scottish throne was the son or a Celtic heiress and the descendant of Scotland's Celtic kings.

Although these incomers brought new ideas of government and national organisation they could not impose them on a subject people but had perforce to adapt them to the ways and outlook of the race into which they were themselves soon absorbed. For that reason there never developed in Scotland at least until very modern times anything like that caste distinction in society which has been so characteristic of England. The practice of democracy came naturally to the people of Scotland since in the fundamental sense of the family all men were equal in blood and dignity if not in power or wealth. England can point to her Magna Carta as the foundation of her liberties but Scotland had no need of a Magna Carta nor of the struggles which led to and followed after it simply because the liberties of her people were never in doubt. The king was not a supreme ruler standing above all law but was the head of the family, *primus inter pares*, who had to obey the law like anyone else and whose power even to impose taxes for the necessary business of Government was severely limited right down to the Union in 1707. That is why Scotland then had no national debt but must needs shoulder her share of England's!

It was for such reasons that in our long discussions in Larachan we constantly reaffirmed our faith, not in any narrow and bitter nationalism, but in the capacity of the Scottish people, given the chance, to reconcile in their politics the freedom and human dignity of every individual with such mass organisation as modern technocracy has made inevitable. We believed that this was the real human problem of our times and that Scotland by virtue of her history, her traditions and even of her size was an ideal testing ground for new solutions.

I have never seen any reason to alter these opinions, but, as I now look back, I can see that the group who then regarded Larachan more or less as their spiritual home were gradually drifting apart in fundamental ideas from that other group in our Party's ranks which strangely enough looked to London and a few dominant members there for leadership. There was, as yet, no outward sign of any divergence but, in a year or two, we were to be divided by what looked like an unbridgeable gulf.

Meantime, however, not only in the north, but all over Scotland we continued to make remarkable headway, and to attract attention sometimes from surprising sources.

CHAPTER NINE

THE GENERAL ELECTION of 1931 took the National Party, as indeed it took everyone in the country, completely by surprise. It was the time of the Gold Standard crisis, of the break-up of Ramsay MacDonald's Labour Government, and of a campaign which, in confusion of issues and in reckless appeal to that spurious thing called British nationalism could only be paralleled by the Khaki Election of 1918.

The National Government which had been formed under Ramsay MacDonald as Prime Minister had failed to gain the support in Parliament of the majority of members of the Parliamentary Labour Party and the Government, therefore, determined to go to the country with the manifest intention of destroying the Labour Party. No programme was put forward by Government spokesmen. Instead, a kind of mass hysteria was whipped up, the Union Jack was wildly waved, and everyone who dared to oppose the Government was denounced as more or less a traitor.

In the result the Labour Party was indeed very nearly destroyed. From having been the largest party in the Commons it was reduced to a mere handful of forty members. Such of its leaders as had refused to join the National Government were nearly all defeated even in what had been regarded as safe seats. Never had there been such a complete collapse of a powerful and well-organised Party.

It might have been thought that, in the whirling rush of such a tide, a puny little craft like the National Party of Scotland would have been altogether overwhelmed. Yet, not only did we survive—we actually improved our position! It had been our intention to put forward twelve candidates

but the election came so suddenly that we could contest only
five seats. These were West Renfrewshire, East Renfrewshire, St. Rollox (Glasgow), East Edinburgh and Inverness-
shire. The candidates were respectively R. E. Muirhead,
W. O. Brown, Elma Campbell, the Rev. T. T. Alexander,
and myself. The results showed that, as against 5 per cent.
of the poll in 1929, we had now risen to an average of nearly
13 per cent. In Inverness-shire, where I had been adopted
as candidate only a month or two before, we gained 14·1 per
cent. the highest percentage of the five seats fought.
Naturally, I was proud of the result, considering that
Inverness-shire is, in area, the largest constituency in Britain,
and that my total election expenses came to less than
£90.

In East Edinburgh there began a flirtation which was soon
to develop almost into a courtship. The *Daily Express* had
been casting around for candidates who would subscribe an
Empire Free Trade pledge. Without any previous consultation with his colleagues our candidate, T. T. Alexander,
suddenly intimated that he would sign it and from that
moment he was Lord Beaverbrook's prime favourite. The
Empire became the big drum in his campaign with Home
Rule a mere patter in the background. Handsome donations
were made to his funds, speakers from London were supplied
and so far as the columns of the *Express* were concerned he
was regarded as practically the only candidate in Scotland.
In spite of that support, East Edinburgh showed the worst
result of all our five contests with only 9·4 per cent. of the
poll and, of course, a lost deposit.

It was in the midst of that General Election campaign
that we scored our first victory. On 24th October, 1931,
Compton Mackenzie was elected Lord Rector of the University of Glasgow despite the opposition of such candidates as
Sir Robert Horne for the Tories, Professor Gilbert Murray

who stood as a Literary Liberal and Mr. Tom Johnston for the Labour Party. It is interesting to note that Sir Oswald Mosley, who had recently formed the New Party, gained only twenty-one votes.

The news of Compton Mackenzie's success reached me while I was campaigning in Skye, and it was with great elation that I announced it on the same evening at a meeting in Dunvegan. Yet in some senses it was a Pyrrhic victory which, owing to the malice of our enemies, did as much harm as good. Mackenzie being a Roman Catholic it was immediately put around by those who envied our growing strength that it was really a Catholic rather than a Nationalist triumph. They went further and insinuated that many of the leading members of the National Party were Catholics and that Home Rule would be synonymous with Rome Rule. When I returned to Inverness I learned that no less a person than the Government candidate himself had gravely informed one of my chief supporters in Glenurquhart that I was both an Irishman and a Catholic. He was suitably astonished when my friend, who was, in fact, a cousin of my mother, pointed up the hill to where she had been born in Craigmore and to Balnain where she got all the schooling she ever had!

However, the lie that our Party was under Catholic control took firm root and spread all over the country like some foul weed. No matter how often it seemed to be uprooted it was sure to sprout again in some other place, and since it always travelled underground it was impossible to stamp it out. The truth, of course, was quite simple. The National Party was completely nonsectarian and took no account of anyone's religion but as might reasonably be expected in Scotland the great majority of its members were good Presbyterians, and, on the National Council, I think Compton Mackenzie himself was the only Catholic.

Personally I have never had any strong religious prejudices, and intolerance has always appeared to me to be one of the most vicious of sins. I could not, therefore, at first fully appreciate how much harm would be done by the Catholic rumours. It had never occurred to me that such prejudices could be unscrupulously and successfully exploited for political reasons, and I had scarcely realised how deep-seated was the fear among a considerable section of the people of Scotland of a Catholic revival.

The fear, of course, seems to me to be quite groundless. I understand that the total Catholic population of Scotland amounts to approximately 650,000 and nearly the whole remaining 4,000,000 to 5,000,000 people in the country are Presbyterian in background and upbringing if not in actual Church membership. It is true that the Catholic population tends to increase slightly more rapidly than the Protestant but, even so, there is no likelihood of any substantial change in the proportions taking place in the foreseeable future.

The real danger to Scotland comes not from the presence of a large religious minority but from the fact that the minority has never really been absorbed into the national life of Scotland. Most of them came into this country from Southern Ireland during the last 100 years at a time when the Scottish people were themselves sadly deficient in national feeling. The result has been that the incomers, deprived by their migration of any natural means of expressing their Irish patriotism, have yet never learned to adopt and feel strongly about their new Scottish nationality. They have, therefore, remained as an undigested mass in our body politic and have created a new and deplorable division in our life. The fact that most of them came from a rural background to work as unskilled labourers in an industrial community to which they were ill adapted has ensured that they and their descendants have lived mainly in squalid, slum conditions as a depressed and despised community with a consequent and inevitable breakdown of morale. All too often the crimes of crude violence which come to the notice of the Courts in places like Glasgow are committed by people with recognisably Irish names and this very fact adds to the initial prejudice which the native Scot might, in any case, have felt against incomers who competed for work and required a less high standard of living. The fault, however, lies largely at our own door. When Scotland has developed a sufficiently healthy national life of her own she will find no difficulty in absorbing the strangers in her midst and turning them into good Scottish citizens. Indeed, in an ever-increasing degree this is already happening and those descendants of the Irish immigrants who, in spite of handicaps, have succeeded in struggling out of the environment to which they were originally condemned, are proving their worth to the nation in many walks of life.

These few paragraphs of digression have, I believe, been necessary if the whole background against which the national movement was growing is to be understood. It remains only to say that Compton Mackenzie's success was in truth a purely Nationalist victory, which is clearly demonstrated by the fact that he gained a larger majority in the Transforthana (or Highland) nation than anywhere else although that particular group of students contains, to all intents and purposes, no Catholics at all. As for Mackenzie himself, although he is indeed a devout Catholic, he has never attempted to introduce religion into politics and has proved his deep attachment to Scotland by making his permanent home here and, in nearly all his later work, writing with some aspect of Scottish life as his theme.

His Rectorial address was a masterly exposition of the philosophy of our nationalism. "Desire the good of your fellow men," he said, "but desire it because you love them, not because a well-fed, well-clad, well-housed creature will be an economic asset to the State."

I had returned from campaigning in the Highlands and was proudly present in St. Andrews Hall when he was installed in office. I heard him say:

"You are luckier than I am, my constituents. You have not to return to Scotland; you are there. And you have not had to maintain your faith through the shifting and deceptive colours of a dream waking from it only in middle age to behold the white and clear and steadfast dawn. You are young at that awakening. There is perhaps at this moment sitting in this hall a student who when ten trienniums shall have passed will stand where I stand now and be triumphant in the golden noon of his country's new life."

Twenty years later, almost to the day, it transpired that I should stand on the same platform wearing the same robe of office, at a time when 2,000,000 people in Scotland were signing the new national Covenant! The only failure in Compton Mackenzie's prophecy was that, although in the interval war had shattered the world, it took only twenty and not thirty years to fulfil.

CHAPTER TEN

In APRIL, 1932, the National Party was again involved in a by-election and, on this occasion, by our intervention we may have unwittingly affected the whole political future in England as well as in Scotland. The Dunbartonshire constituency had fallen vacant and although in the Labour collapse of 1931 it had been won by the Tories it had formerly been regarded as a safe Labour seat. The National Government was beginning to lose its popularity and it seemed possible that the 1931 result might be reversed. The Labour Party, therefore, nominated as their candidate, Mr. Tom Johnston, who had lost his seat in Stirlingshire a few months before. The Government candidate was Commander Cochrane, later appointed Governor-General of Burma, and there was a Communist candidate Hugh McIntyre who was a well-known local County Councillor.

At first we hesitated to put forward a candidate of our own. Tom Johnston had already proved himself to be one of the most sincere Home Rulers in the Labour Party and nobody could have any doubt about his staunch Scottish patriotism. But we had pledged ourselves to oppose, wherever possible, all candidates sponsored by the English controlled parties and we felt constrained to stand by that pledge. We therefore entered the fight with Robert Gray as our candidate.

I think it was one of the most keenly contested by-elections I have ever been involved in, which was understandable considering how high were the stakes. The Labour Party in Parliament had not only been reduced to paltry numbers but it also lacked any outstanding leadership. More to fill the gap than anything else George Lansbury, an ageing Christian Socialist and Pacifist who was out of sympathy with the times, had been elected Leader but it was clear that whenever a more suitable man should make his way back into the House of Commons Lansbury would make way for him. The obvious person for the job was Tom Johnston. He had been Lord Privy Seal in the late Labour Government and had finally been entrusted with the immense task of dealing with the problem of unemployment. His prestige in his party was high and there can be little doubt that had he gone back to Parliament he would soon have been made Leader of the Opposition instead of the choice falling on the then little-known Clement Attlee.

To the Government also the by-election was important. It was the first since the General Election, the seat was by no means secure, and it was important for their prestige to retain it. The consequence was that both the major parties brought their whole strength to bear in the constituency and vied with each other in producing nationally known speakers.

For our part we were by now well-seasoned campaigners and were nothing daunted by the big guns firing over our heads and occasionally aiming a shot in our direction. Robert Gray, who had begun so haltingly as a chairman in Camlachie was now a first-rate speaker with a turn of humour which was all his own and which thoroughly endeared him to his Clydeside audiences. We had developed a shuttle-service technique for the supply of speakers to meetings, with the result that when the other parties were holding two or three meetings every evening we could cope with five or six, though we had far fewer trained speakers to call upon. As usual, our meetings were well attended and the genuine interest shown in our propaganda far exceeded the actual voting strength which we could muster.

Even in voting strength, however, we did very well. We

polled more than 6,000 votes, an equivalent of 13·5 per cent. of all votes cast. The Government retained the seat by a majority over Labour of only 2,000 and it was clear that we had held the balance of power and prevented a Labour victory. There is no doubt that we thus altered the history of the Labour Party in Parliament, which might have followed very different courses had Tom Johnston become its leader.

Of course, I do not know whether Mr. Johnston cherished such ambitions for himself, though rumour widely had it that he was grievously disappointed by his defeat. However that may be, he never reproached us nor did he waver in his support for Home Rule. Later, in the dark years of the war, he was to become Secretary of State for Scotland and to render many invaluable services to his country and now he is, with little doubt, the one man above all others who has contributed to the rebuilding of Scotland's economy.

I now believe that we were mistaken in opposing him in Dunbartonshire, but who knows whether, if he had become Leader of the Labour Party, he would ever have had the time or opportunity even granting the inclination to do so much for Scotland.

The obvious influence which we had exerted in Dunbartonshire called forth increasing attention to the National Party from all quarters and not least from the Press. At that time a considerable Press war was being waged in Scotland. The *Daily Express* had opened a fully equipped Glasgow office and was now printing its Scottish edition there. A complete editorial staff was installed and every effort was being made to establish it as a Scottish national daily and not a mere local edition. Its principal rival as a popular paper was the *Daily Record* which had long been firmly established in Scotland and had by now with its companion the *Evening News* come under the control of the Berry group. The Editor-in-chief of the Berry papers in Glasgow was David

R. Anderson, a journalist of real genius, and a very accomplished artist as well. He was small and dark, of Napoleonic appearance and full of energy. To all intents and purposes he had a completely free hand in running his newspapers and he entered into the battle with the *Daily Express* with furious zest. By personal inclination he was something of a Nationalist himself and he saw quite clearly that the only way to keep the *Daily Record's* end up was to emphasise on every page that it was a really Scottish national newspaper and not a mere offshoot from London.

The *Express* fought back on the same front. Was not Lord Beaverbrook a Canadian Scot, son of a Scottish Presbyterian minister, and did his aunts not still live in Bathgate in West Lothian? Surely that was sufficient answer to the claims of the Berrys from Wales that theirs was a Scottish newspaper. And to make the claims of the *Express* still more explicit the Scottish Editor began to give unprecedented publicity to the activities of the National Party of Scotland.

It was early in this contest that, as Honorary Secretary of the National Party, I found myself unexpectedly invited to meet Lord Beaverbrook himself. I was suitably impressed when I was asked to call on him in the Royal Suite of the Central Hotel in Glasgow, and I vividly remember my impressions and almost every detail of my conversation with him.

Although he is even smaller in stature than myself and no one could call his appearance prepossessing he has undoubtedly that gift of powerful personality which dominates other men. I had often seen photographs and caricatures of him, and I had my own preconceived and ultra-cautious ideas about him, but when I met him he seemed so different from any representation and he greeted me with such an air of friendly welcome that my defences began to crumble right away. Having been warned by all my friends to use a

"long spoon when supping with the devil" I found myself
instead vastly enjoying his company and fascinated, though
not altogether overwhelmed, by his charm.

He talked to me in an intimate way about his Scottish
family connections and his early life in his father's manse in
Canada. He assured me that it had always been one of his
ambitions to found a truly Scottish newspaper and that the
last thing he desired was merely to palm off on the Scottish
people a reprint of a London daily. Could I suggest anything
which would help him?

I ventured to point out that in fact the *Daily Express* was
well-known to be a London newspaper and that unless he
could change its name in some way so as to emphasise that he
really meant to found something new he would find it difficult to convince his Scottish readers. Moreover, no one in
Scotland wanted to read advertisements for London cinemas
which still appeared in the *Express* and it would be much
better to give space even at lower charge to entertainments
in Scotland. Finally, and here I put in a word for my
own point of view, such was the rising tide of national
feeling in Scotland that unless his paper would join in giving
expression to it he would find it difficult to establish it firmly
here.

To all of this he appeared to give vigorous consent. I
cannot say whether or not it was cause and effect but within
a week or two the word "Scottish" was used for the first time
in the name of the *Express* and under its title streamer
appeared the caption "Founded by Lord Beaverbrook."
More and more attention was paid to the National Party
and thereafter for about a year I was called upon to meet
Beaverbrook and some of the members of his Scottish staff
nearly every time he visited Glasgow. On one occasion I
suggested that it would be a fine thing if the *Express* would
organise a straw ballot on Home Rule in Glasgow. The idea

was that various people should be invited to state the case
for and against in the paper and that on an appointed day
polling stations should be set up at strategic points throughout the city and the citizens be asked to show their preference
on a simply-worded ballot paper.

The suggestion was taken up with enthusiasm by Lord
Beaverbrook and his staff in Albion Street, and it proved
both from their and my point of view to be a great success.
No less than 116,000 people recorded votes and of that
total 112,000 favoured Home Rule and only 4,000 were
against. I believe the test was taken fairly and counted
accurately, and, of course, it was a great feather in our caps.
It seemed that before long we should command the overwhelming support of public opinion.

It was at this time that Lord Beaverbrook called for me
to discuss certain suggestions which he thought would be of
value to the National Party. He had already openly proclaimed his support for our movement in a letter which he
published in the *Daily Express* on 14th July, 1932, in these
terms:

"As for Scottish Nationalism I am, of course, strongly in
favour of that movement. It is a sound movement and it is
not made unsound because some of its supporters express
extreme views. The movement that has no extremists has no
promise of development and growth.

"Scottish Nationalism would give Scotland control of her
domestic policies while securing her in her present share of
Imperial concerns. That is a splendid project. It would
bind the Empire more closely together. It would ensure that
closer and more efficient attention was paid to the Scottish
administration. No one will deny that the Scottish race is
better able to look after its own affairs than any Parliament
sitting in Westminster. . . ."

I believed (and still believe) that he was perfectly sincere in that forthright declaration and my mind was, therefore, open to consider any proposal he might put before us. In a long discussion he cross-examined me very thoroughly on the state of our organisation, our funds and our preparedness in the constituencies. While I did my best to put a good face on things I realised that I was not his only informant and that without any revelations from me he had a very shrewd appreciation of our weaknesses. Ours was, of course, an organisation of amateurs and I doubt whether any of us would have changed that status even if we could. We all had a hatred and distrust of a "political machine" and for that very reason we failed to appreciate the very formidable power of the professionally organised parties. We knew that they were soulless, that their members lacked any real enthusiasm except for their own advancement, and that we could far outdo them in popular appeal. We failed to realise that the advent of universal suffrage, thrusting the power of the vote on thousands of politically illiterate electors, had made the evolution of the party machine inevitable. One of the problems which has not yet been solved in any democracy is how to reconcile equality of citizenship with the natural leadership of men of independent mind.

Lord Beaverbrook, with his experience of building up a newspaper to a circulation of 3,000,000 or 4,000,000, knew much better than I did how important the minutiae of political registers, card indices and street canvasses could be. When he had heard my answers to all his questions he shook his head:

"I'm afraid, my boy," he said, "you have no chance whatever in Parliamentary elections. You've done far better already than you had any right to expect but you'll not get much further. Why don't you try local government elections, even on a narrow front? Party organisation counts for far less in local affairs. You should turn the next Municipal

Election in Glasgow and Edinburgh into a miniature General Election on Home Rule."

I waited noncommittally for I could sense that he was working up to some theme which really interested him.

"If you could win every seat in Glasgow Corporation for Scottish Nationalism," he continued, "you wouldn't need to wait long before both the Tories and the Socialists would swallow your programme. Why ram your heads against them in Parliamentary elections where they have all the advantages? Get at them locally, on local problems where you can advocate a non-party approach, and you'll take them by surprise."

I pointed out that we had already contested one or two local authority elections but he waved me aside:

"One or two!" he exclaimed. "That's not dramatic! That won't call attention to your party. What you must do is fight every municipal ward in Glasgow next November and make a real issue of it."

When I protested that we had quite inadequate funds for such a programme, he went on:

"You'll get the funds when you strike the people's imagination. Don't worry about that. I'll contribute myself and in a big way. But your Party must fight in a big way. There's no use nibbling at it."

By this time he had really warmed up to his subject and was talking as though I was altogether too timid and moderate a Nationalist who needed to be prodded on to activity. I could see very well the real force of his argument and if it could be done I was willing to try his idea. I told him so, and he seemed pleased that he had been able to spare something from his immensely fertile mind for the country of his origin. We parted as the best of friends and, as I left him at the door of his suite, he impulsively grasped my hand in both of his and said:

"God bless you, John. This is a big work you've set your hand to and some day your dream for Scotland will come true. I have many other interests but I'll always spare a thought for this old nation."

I have often heard it said that Beaverbrook is insincere, that anything he takes up is a mere stunt to boost his sales or his own reputation. Yet I believe I saw him at that moment, with all his guards down, as a perfectly simple, sentimental Colonial Scot speaking quite truly from his heart and giving the blessing of a busy man to something which he felt was wholly desirable but not for him to achieve.

CHAPTER ELEVEN

WHILE BEAVERBROOK was thus identifying himself with the land of his fathers, David Anderson continued to fight valiantly for the claims of the *Daily Record*. Anderson was a shrewd man, and he turned the limitations which were imposed by his owners on his own exuberant nationalism to good account. He knew, probably better than did anyone in the *Express*, that the National Party was handicapped by the intransigence of some of its most vociferous followers and that middle-class opinion, while vaguely Scottish, was far too timid (or too sensible) to swallow the anti-English and absurdly introspectionist sentiments which were very often voiced from our platform.

He, therefore, took it upon himself to encourage through the *Daily Record* every more moderate expression of national feeling while, of course, still insisting that the *Record* was the only real national newspaper in Scotland. He reckoned that if Beaverbrook could swallow extremists, the *Record* would spew them forth and he conducted his policy with very considerable skill.

A quite fortuitous circumstance gave him his cue. In June, 1932, a large and prosperous Unionist Association controlling the safe seat of Cathcart in Glasgow suddenly severed its connection with the Tory Party and declared that it stood for Scottish Home Rule and Imperial Federation. The breakaway was led by a well-known Glasgow lawyer, Kevan McDowall, whose tense and high-strung energy made it an immediate and serious threat to the complacency of Tory Headquarters. The *Record* gave the utmost publicity to the Cathcart rebels and held them up to admiration as a responsible and moderate group although in fact there was very little difference between the policy announced in their manifesto and that of the National Party.

Kevan McDowall was a tireless letter-writer and he began to bombard leading people throughout Scotland requesting messages of support for his action. He met with a fair measure of success. Sir Alexander MacEwen of Inverness, the Duke of Montrose, Andrew Dewar Gibb (later Professor of Law at Glasgow University and then a barrister practising in London who had already published *Scotland in Eclipse*, a useful handbook of Scottish grievances), many leading Churchmen and local government personalities intimated their approval of his aims.

Recognising the existence of so widespread a group of Home Rulers who none-the-less spurned the National Party, the *Daily Record* placed itself at the van of what it called the Moderates and summoned a Conference of them. There was much blowing of trumpets about "No Separation" and the "Empire", and, before the Conference met, the *Record* took the unusual course of addressing a full-length questionnaire spread across its middle page, to the National Party.

This enormous publicity was, of course, all to the good and far more than anything we had ever expected. We replied to the questionnaire in as conciliatory terms as we could and through the instrumentality of Neil Gunn in Inverness I had several friendly discussions with Sir Alexander MacEwen to see whether there was any real gulf of opinion between us.

Sir Alexander had been for a number of years Provost of Inverness, and while he was nominally a member of the Liberal Party, he had for long devoted his whole energies to local and Highland affairs. He was a man far above the ordinary run of small-town Provosts, with a keen intellect, a wide cultural background and a gift of natural eloquence which would have placed him high in any political Party. He had now, along with the Duke of Montrose, come to be regarded as the leader of moderate Scottish opinion and the high respect in which he was held all over Scotland made it certain that many who would otherwise have been apathetic would take a new and livelier interest in the National Movement.

He was a shy and reserved man and since I was very young and conscious of my inexperience I would have found it difficult to talk freely to him had it not been for Neil Gunn who acted as intermediary and for whom the Provost had the highest admiration and affection. With Neil's help the barriers of reserve on one hand and diffidence on the other were soon broken down and I found not only that there was no fundamental difference of opinion between us but also that his whole attitude to the Scottish question corresponded far more nearly to my own than did that of some of my colleagues in the National Party.

As an outcome of these talks, all unknown to David Anderson who was mothering the forthcoming Moderate Conference like an anxious hen, Sir Alexander prepared a draft statement of the Moderates' aims which he submitted to me and was flexible enough to alter here and there when I could suggest modifications which would avoid an open challenge to the more intransigent members of the National Party. In due course his statement was unanimously approved by the Conference and almost immediately thereafter the *Daily Record's* enthusiasm for the Moderates began to wane. By declaring that they wanted a Scottish Parliament with sovereign authority in Scottish affairs, including finance, while at the same time recognising the need for joint United Kingdom machinery to deal with such affairs as defence and foreign policy, they went far beyond the limits which Anderson had set for his aims.

Contrary to my own hopes, however, they had not succeeded by this bold declaration in satisfying the "old guard" in the National Party, particularly most of the leading members of what had been the Scots National League.

There was, in fact, a subtle and scarcely definable dividing line which separated one section of Nationalists from another and which to this day has persisted. It had little really to do with moderation or extremism or with statements of policy. It was rather a difference in mental approach which made itself felt in discussion of any question. On the one hand there was what I can only call a kind of cantankerousness, as though those who displayed it felt themselves, however unconsciously, to belong to a defeated and conquered nation and must, therefore, always stand on their dignity and look out for every slight. They seemed to me to look at Scotland through green spectacles and despite a complete lack of historical parallel to identify the Irish struggle with their own. On the other hand there were those whose nationalism was a perfectly healthy desire for a better form of union with England than that which had been freely negotiated in 1707, and who never, either consciously or unconsciously thought of Scotland as having anything other than an equal status with England, however unfortunately the incorporating Union of Parliaments might reflect itself in modern Scottish life. I am glad to say, and I think it is significant of the temper of the Scottish people, that it is the latter state of mind which, in the long run, has predominated in the National Movement.

A common enthusiasm had at first supplied the emulsifying element which within the National Party had fused two such different types but the emergence of the new Moderate group put a severe strain on our capacity for agreement. Despite the accommodating nature of the statement drawn up by Sir Alexander MacEwen many of our leading members continued to hurl abuse at him and all his colleagues and I came to be regarded with suspicion merely because I was prepared to talk with him.

As a result nothing more could then be done to secure a broad-based unity of action and, in due course, the Duke of Montrose, Sir Alexander MacEwen, Dewar Gibb, Kevan McDowall and others banded themselves together to form an entirely new organisation, the Scottish Party, with the avowed intention of rivalling the National Party in the political field. I and many of my friends were grievously disappointed but we could do nothing more than bide our time until we could make wiser counsels prevail.

In spite of all this concern with split-hair policy-making and the wrangles to which it gave rise at our Council meetings and Conferences we seemed for the time being to continue to make good progress. In September, 1932, Lord Dalziel of Kirkcaldy who had until recently been proprietor of *Reynolds's Newspaper*, decided to join the National Party and signalised that step by asking me to organise a public meeting in Dumfries at which he could declare his allegiance. He was an important capture and I went out of my way to nourish his new-found nationalism. Years before, as Sir Henry Dalziel, M.P. for Kirkcaldy, he had played an important part in politics. He was one of the men who had helped to bring Asquith down and push Lloyd George to the top in 1916, and ever since those days had been a close friend of Lord Beaverbrook. In view, therefore, of his political connections and great wealth it seemed to me that he could render invaluable services to the National Party and I did everything possible to make his meeting in Dumfries a success.

Fortune favoured us, and despite a bitterly cold night we had a packed hall. I had no idea whether His Lordship was a competent speaker or not and was not even very sure that he fully understood what our aims were. I need not have worried. He spoke with all the skill of a thoroughly seasoned politician and, despite his advancing years and failing health, was both a dignified and vigorous figure on the platform. He told his audience that years ago, as a young Liberal M.P., he had been a strong advocate of Home Rule and that now in his old age he had returned to Scotland to see his dream come true. The enthusiasm of the meeting obviously delighted him and I felt sure that he was now firmly settled in our fold.

On the following morning, back in Glasgow, I received an angry telephone call from him from his home in Borgue. Had I read the leading article in the *Glasgow Herald* commenting on his speech? He was furious with it and with Sir Robert Bruce its Editor. Long ago Bruce and he had started life together as brash young lobby correspondents in Westminster. They had represented competing newspapers and the rivalry which then began between them had apparently continued as a hearty mutual dislike.

All this came pouring over to me on the telephone together with many threats as to what His Lordship would do with the *Glasgow Herald*. He proposed to leave Borgue immediately by car and asked me to book him rooms in the Central Hotel and meet him there as soon as he arrived in Glasgow.

He reached town in the early afternoon and when I met him he was pacing the floor of his room impatiently, still obviously in a fine rage with the *Glasgow Herald*. Almost his first words to me were, "John, have you a good stockbroker?"

It was only very recently that I had set up in business as a solicitor in a one roomed office adjacent to our Party rooms in Glasgow. My clientele was not of the class that normally required the services of a stockbroker and my own resources were not such as to encourage speculation on the Exchange. I was, therefore, slightly taken aback and answered with a very hesitant "Yes," rather than disclose the emptiness of my cupboard.

"Ring him up, then, and buy all the shares you can in the *Glasgow Herald*!"

My face must have betrayed my surprise.

"Do it right now," he said. "I'm going to the next share-holders' meeting to make hell about that leading article."

I had a vague memory of the names of one or two stock-brokers from the days of my apprenticeship and with no relish for my task I rang up one of them, who had doubtless never heard of me before. I gave my name and professional address and then went right on with my enquiry.

"Do you think it's possible that there might be some Outram shares on the market? I have a client who is inter-ested." The broker answered suavely, "Well, that's very strange. You know they seldom come on the market but I have a packet of 4,000 on offer to-day. They're standing at £4 which makes a deal at £16,000. Do you think your client would be interested—and, eh, who is your client, by the way?"

"Excuse me a moment," I said, and covered the mouth-piece with my hand, quite confident that this would be the end of the whole miserable enquiry. I turned to Lord Dalziel and whispered, "He can get 4,000 shares but they're valued at £16,000. He wants to know who is interested!"

"Buy them right now," said Dalziel. "Tell him it's Lord Dalziel of Kirkcaldy and the quicker he tells Bruce the better!"

I spoke into the telephone again and carried out my instructions. When I had given the name of my client a new note of respect crept into the stockbroker's voice. "Very good, Mr. MacCormick, thanks ever so much. You'll write and confirm, won't you! Lord Dalziel of Kirkcaldy, didn't you say? Very good, very good indeed."

My own strictly private mental comment was perhaps not dissimilar. Our movement had, at last, found a man who, without the flicker of an eyelid, could spend £16,000 on a mere angry whim!

CHAPTER TWELVE

IN THE AUTUMN of 1932, so apparent had become the advance of the Nationalist Movement that its opponents could no longer treat it lightly as a thing either to be sneered at or ignored. Suddenly without the slightest preliminary rumble, a very modest volcano erupted in anger against us. The occasion was the publication of a manifesto warning the people of Scotland against Home Rule, and signed by some 400 of the leading reactionaries in Scotland. The first signatory was the late Lord Maclay, a wealthy shipowner, and there followed him four dukes, five earls, fifteen barons and a host of industrialists of the type who had swept across central Scotland like a blast from the fiery furnace, leaving in their wake instead of the loveliness which had been there such mean and leafless scars as Coatbridge, Motherwell and Bellshill.

They were, with some honourable exceptions, the kind of men who, having either inherited or ruthlessly exploited the wealth of their native country, had then invested both their money and their dreams of stuffed respectability elsewhere. The height of their ambition was to send their sons to Eton and the depth of their fear was that any change in the Constitution would endanger their money bags. The *Glasgow Herald* hailed them as the leaders of industry in Scotland but their leadership, however profitable for themselves, had ended in a quagmire of unemployment, emigration, slums and mass tuberculosis! The enterprise of their predecessors, however roughshod it may have been, had long since deserted them and so long as gilt-edged securities gave them sufficient affluence they had neither the interest nor the stimulus to keep our industries up to date. They were about as timid a set of "leaders" as anyone could have found and well deserved the by-name "Ragman's Roll" by which they soon became universally known.

The manifesto was a very damp squib and little more has ever been heard of it. Indeed, I imagine that a good many of those who were persuaded to sign it now much regret their folly and hope with all their hearts that no one will ever quote it against them.

It is, however, worth mentioning not only because it indicates that our comparative success was already arousing active opposition, but also because it contained a series of fatuous arguments which, without knowledge of their source, have often been repeated. The fundamental thesis, upon which all else was built, was that Scotland was a very poor country which could only exist in modern conditions by kind permission of the English and with the help of occasional subventions from the London Treasury. The truth, of course, was easily demonstrated from official publications, which showed that, relatively to population, Scotland produced far more food, power, steel, machinery and means of transport than did England and had, as well, more money in the bank than did England. This was to say nothing of the almost innumerable inventions which had originated in Scottish minds nurtured in Scottish schools and universities wholly maintained out of the Scottish purse which had made the modern technological revolution possible.

The further major contention of the manifesto was that any measure of self-government in Scotland would upset the free flow of trade between the two countries and would thus impoverish them both. No evidence was adduced to show that this would be so and the obvious examples to the contrary such as the self-governing states of the U.S.A. or the Commonwealth of Australia were ignored. The document, in short, was not so much an argument as a statement of prejudice and fear dressed up to sound like a weighty warning to the Scottish people. It gave the speakers of the National Party useful platform ammunition and, in the long run, did more good than harm to the Home Rule cause.

Meantime, we were ourselves in difficulties over the forthcoming Municipal Elections. I had endeavoured to persuade our National Council to take up Lord Beaverbrook's suggestion but there were strong differences of opinion about the wisdom of contesting local authority elections and many objections to our doing anything suggested by one of the Press lords. In the end we put up only a handful of candidates in Edinburgh and Glasgow, and, while most of them fared reasonably well, very few were elected. From that time Beaverbrook's interest in us began to wane and very soon he set out in Scotland on his own campaign against Baldwin. In a series of widely publicised meetings he never once reverted to his former statement of faith in Nationalism, and, while the *Express* continued to pat us occasionally on the back, it was clear that the courtship was at an end. I never met Beaverbrook again until, in 1950, I almost stumbled against him on the deck of the *Queen Mary*—but that is another story!

The final break with him was soon to come. Early in the New Year of 1933, a vacancy occurred in the East Fife Parliamentary Division and we, of course, welcomed the opportunity to fly our colours again. With some difficulty we succeeded in persuading Eric Linklater to accept nomination as our candidate. He had very recently won considerable fame with the publication of *Juan in America* which was by way of being a best-seller and our announcement that he had agreed to stand as a Nationalist candidate was hailed on all hands as a considerable feather in our cap.

The by-election which followed was one of the most extraordinary in which I have ever taken part. The Government

candidate was J. Henderson Stuart who had, until very
recently, been a leading member of the Liberal Party but
now went forward as a National Liberal. In high dudgeon
at what they regarded as a betrayal the Liberal Party then
nominated David Keir, a rising young journalist who loudly
proclaimed his support for Home Rule. Then to everyone's
astonishment Beaverbrook established an Empire Free Trade
committee in the constituency and secured the services of a
well-known local farmer, J. L. Anderson who stood under the
title of Agricultural and Empire Unionist. The Labour
nominee was Joseph Westwood who later became Secretary
of State for Scotland in Mr. Attlee's first Cabinet.

The three daily newspapers which were then actively
endeavouring to increase their Scottish circulation entered
the fray in an unprecedented manner—the *Express* for
Anderson, the *News Chronicle* for Keir and the *Daily Herald*
for Westwood. Loudspeaker vans, newspaper posters and
hordes of journalists appeared all over the constituency, and,
in due course, Lord Beaverbrook himself with a complete
staff of star reporters, secretaries and speakers arrived from
London and encamped in Rusack's Hotel on the links at St.
Andrews.

Eric Linklater had also taken up his abode there and, on
the many occasions, when, in that bitterly cold and foggy
January, it was impossible to return to Glasgow after late
meetings our Nationalist speakers, too, made Rusack's their
headquarters. The result, of course, was that, after hurling
abuse at each other from the hustings, the rival sides met
together for long and friendly *ceilidhs* after hours.

The Beaverbrook circus included some of the most lively
talkers I have ever met. There was Bill Barkley whose job it
was to report Beaverbrook's speeches, with plenty of local
colour and journalistic varnish thrown in. His muttered
protests at being dragged all over East Fife on icy roads to

write what he could as well have written without ever being near a meeting were more eloquent even than the speeches he reported. George Malcolm Thomson, who, I think, at that time, was Beaverbrook's private secretary and journalistic adviser, was also in the team. Unknown to his chief he was, and had long been, a keen member of the National Party and the author of much of our literature. On one occasion some months previously Beaverbrook had gravely introduced him to me as a distinguished Scottish historian, little knowing that I had spent many a happy evening with him and his lovely Norwegian wife in their home in Hampstead. His quiet and cynical humour as he now contemplated his own situation in the van of the Agricultural Unionist and Empire crusade or crossed swords with Linklater in mock duel was to an unseasoned youngster like myself a source of rich delight.

Most vivid in my memory of those late nights, however, is Viscount Castlerosse whose function in the team of electioneers was somewhat obscure but who presided over our midnight revelries with unquenchable charm. He was an immense, ruddy, heavy-jowled man who, with very little trimming might easily have passed for a portrait of Henry VIII. He knew everything about the good things of life and his capacity for spiced gossip was endless. For some reason he and I became fast friends and often when sleep had overcome all the others he would regale me with rich tales of life in high society and even with his father's memories of the less seemly side of the Victorian Court. I think he had rarely come across anyone so unsophisticated as I was and he took delight in giving me instruction on the ways of the world he knew so well. Although I never met him again after that hectic campaign I felt a real and sudden sense of loss when afterwards I learned of his death.

These and the other members there of Beaverbrook's

circus were brilliant men, holding top jobs in their profession and well aware of their own high price in the Fleet Street market. They were or pretended to be highly cynical about the campaign which they were running but they were strangely united in one thing—their intense personal loyalty to their chief. They were like a group of schoolboys who would hate to admit it but had both an awe and an affection for their Headmaster.

Throughout the election Beaverbrook was suffering considerably from asthma and although he contrived to speak at two or three meetings every day he retired to his own rooms in Rusack's whenever his meetings were over. Regularly, however, as the night wore on his soft-footed valet would appear at the glass swing doors of the lounge and summon one or other of the revellers to the presence of the master. There would be a sudden pause in our laughter and a quick look round to see who was this time required. It was as though they all uneasily awaited the judgement of the god upstairs!

Apart from these nights of relaxation our Nationalist campaign was a strenuous one indeed. Three or four speakers would leave Glasgow late every afternoon and motor 100 miles or so often through thick fog and always on ice-bound roads to key points in the constituency. Frequently we were late and inexperienced local speakers had to hold the fort till our arrival. The public, bemused by a welter of candidates who all declared their firm belief in Home Rule, listened coldly to our blandishments and, unlike the audiences to which we had by now become accustomed, seldom evinced any sign of enthusiasm.

Linklater himself, who had entered the campaign full of fight, soon began to show signs of bafflement. His style of oratory, somewhat heavy and lightened only by careful wit and calculated humour, was not of the kind best suited to the stolid townsfolk of the East Neuk of Fife. He was not the kind of person to suffer fools gladly and the many gaps in our organisation annoyed him intensely. It became difficult for him to conceal his contempt for the electorate and, although he loyally continued to expound our case, I am sure that, long before the campaign was over, he had decided that politics was not in his line of country.

In one respect his attitude of bored indifference served us ill. With some difficulty I had persuaded Lord Dalziel to visit the constituency and speak at one or two meetings. Unfortunately, he was not impressed by Linklater and something akin to a mutual dislike was at once apparent between them. Thereafter, His Lordship bombarded me with the somewhat impractical advice that, having made a show at fighting in the constituency, we should withdraw at the last moment before nomination day. I suppose that, like the shrewd politician he was, he had a prescience of the result but he failed to reckon with the uproar which would have followed in our Party if we had taken any such course. From that time, however, his interest in us began to wane and when he died two years later he willed a fortune of £750,000 to the Chancellor of the Exchequer. The National Party could well have done with even a small fraction of that sum!

In the end, East Fife was a severe blow to all our rising hopes. When the result was declared on 2nd February, 1933, our candidate was at the foot of the poll with only 1,083 votes and the lowest percentage we had gained since 1929. The Independent Liberal was next in ascending order with 2,296 followed by Beaverbrook's nominee with 4,404. The Government candidate went in with a majority of 9,000 over Labour and a poll which more than equalled that of his four opponents put together.

CHAPTER THIRTEEN

THE RESULT OF the East Fife election, so disappointing after a succession of forward steps, naturally caused much heart-searching in our ranks. There were those who said that it was the Nemesis for our attempts to state our case reasonably enough to prevent the formation of the Scottish Party. The others (and I was one of them myself) believed that we had not properly reflected the mood of national opinion and had spent far too much energy in wrangling about the precise terms in which we should state our aims.

Certainly the Scottish Party had done nothing to help us in the election. They had sent a questionnaire to all the candidates and four of them answered with unqualified affirmatives. The Scottish Party, therefore, advised the electors that there was nothing to choose between these four and thus considerably complicated our electioneering task. Yet I could hardly blame them for their stupid neutrality. There had been so many people in the ranks of the National Party who poured contempt upon them and spurned them with more self-righteousness than was shown to our most reactionary opponents that they could hardly be expected now to rush to our support.

It seemed to me and to many others in the National Party that we could not afford to allow the Scottish Party to continue in its separate existence. It was led by men whose names were far better known to the public than were any of ours and who commanded the respect which is always given, whether due or not, to rank and position. Moreover, I had a feeling that while many of our countrymen were dissatisfied with the state of the Union they desired not to break it up but to reform it. The spokesmen of the Scottish Party were far more nearly representative of that broad opinion than were some of our own leaders, most of whose lives had been spent in London and whose Scotland was more of a nostalgic dream than the reality with which we must contend. I therefore made up my mind that even at the cost of shedding some of the intransigents, for whom, as individuals, I had the highest admiration and respect, we must seek to amalgamate the two organisations.

The first step necessary to take in pursuance of that policy was to secure a restatement of our aims such that it could form a basis of negotiation. But it was no easy task to draw up any kind of statement which was at all likely both to secure the approval of a delegate conference of the National Party and to play the part of an olive branch to our rivals. It would, I think, have been impossible to do so but for the help of Tom Gibson who after some natural hesitation decided to advance the cause of unity. He had a considerable understanding of the mind of the "sea-green incorruptibles" which in some measure he shared, but he was also fully alive to the practicalities of politics in Scotland. With great care and in the hope that we should offend as few susceptibilities as possible we cut down our demands to what we thought was the essential minimum and presented them as a statement of policy to our National Council. By a narrow majority and after much bitter argument the statement was approved for submission to a Delegate Conference to be held in May, 1933.

The Conference packed a fairly large hall in Glasgow and it was sheer pandemonium. Our Chairman, R. E. Muirhead, was never a master of procedure and in that long day of heated recrimination and violent abuse he became so confused in his rulings that no one could be quite sure what had been decided. The London and Edinburgh delegates were the most vitriolic opponents of anything which they called compromise. To my astonishment they launched bitter personal attacks against myself and utterly condemned me on a score of self-contradictory grounds. I had dallied with the Press, I had talked with Sir Alexander MacEwen, I had coaxed Lord Dalziel on to our platform, I had induced Linklater to stand in East Fife and so on. In the end, at nearly midnight, the Conference was adjourned having, as far as anyone could judge, taken two entirely opposite decisions. The revised statement of aims was approved but a supplementary resolution authorising official talks with the Scottish Party was rejected! The only thing which was unanimously agreed was that we should meet again to fight it out some other day.

The Inverness delegates to the Conference had taken rooms in the Royal Hotel and late though the hour was they invited the other leading proponents of negotiation with the Scottish Party to join them there. After much discussion we decided that there was only one effective course open to us. We must endeavour to expel from the Party the leading members of the London Branch, Angus Clark and W. D. McColl, disband the branch and wind up the Edinburgh Area Council. It seemed a drastic step to contemplate and one which might quite possibly destroy the Party altogether. Yet we calculated, and the event proved us right, that among the extreme element there was no natural power of cohesion and if once we could be rid of them we need not fear that they could successfully set up any rival organisation. On the other hand, if we forced through a union with the Scottish Party while they still remained among us they would be a constant thorn in our flesh and an endless source of dissension. Already for nearly twelve months we had dissipated our energies on internal disputes and our failure in East Fife was largely due to that dissipation. Tom Gibson had known and been friendly with these people ever since the foundation of the Scots National League in 1923 but, albeit with natural reluctance, he fully concurred in our decision and played an important part in carrying it out.

It may seem now to the reader of these notes that the issues involved were trivial or that our very young Party was far too small to excite so much concern among its members. Yet we believed that we were dealing with questions of the utmost importance to the future of Scotland. We were emotionally involved in our attachment to the Party which we had all helped to found and we could not lightly risk its future.

The adjourned Conference, before which the motion of expulsion was put, was held in Glasgow in October, 1933. Both sides of the dispute had canvassed the now numerous branches of the Party with the result that there was a full turn-out of several hundred delegates. The atmosphere was tense from the moment the Chairman rose with the usual formalities to open the meeting. As Secretary of the Party I sat at his right hand and I looked at the rows of people in front of me wondering who were hostile and who were friendly. I was probably, by a good many years, the youngest person there but I felt that for some reason I had become the focus either for intense and vituperative enmity or for an almost unreasoning loyalty. I believed that the decisions which were to be taken were make or break not only for myself but for a movement whose inner purpose was to reverse 200 years of history and to put forgotten Scotland back on the map of the world.

Every delegate there must also have felt the same sense of importance in the occasion. There were no loud and angry scenes, no interruption of speeches, no points of order to distract attention. The meeting was sitting in judgement and behaved accordingly.

Parliamentary Election, 1929—Camlachie Division

SCOTLAND FIRST.

JOHN MacCORMICK : the Man who Trusts You.

"Ye see the distress that we are in, how Jerusalem lieth waste, and the gates thereof are burned with fire: come, and let us build up the walls of Jerusalem, that we be no more a reproach."—Nehemiah ii. 17.

Campaign leaflet for the Parliamentary Election, 1929

The National Party of Scotland

AT WESTMINSTER

SCOTLAND IS A SOVEREIGN NATION, and while it will make use of the existing political machinery, the National Party of Scotland does not acknowledge the right of the Westminster Parliament to set limits to, or to define the form of Scottish National Self-Government.

SELF-GOVERNMENT BILL

The National Party will, therefore, present at Westminster a Self-Government Bill covering the following points:—(1) The termination of the incorporating Union with England, (2) The summoning by the King of a Scottish Constituent Assembly to frame the Scottish Constitution for approval of the Scottish People, (3) The continuation of the existing laws until repealed by the Scottish Legislative Assembly, and (4) The appointment of an Executive of that Assembly to treat with England on common matters.

CONSTITUENCY AFFAIRS

The National Party recognises the right of a constituency to expect that its representative will give adequate attention to local affairs affecting the constituency, and National Members will be free to press the desires of their constituents on such matters.

ECONOMIC AND SOCIAL MATTERS

While full justice in respect of Scotland's economic and social affairs will never be obtained at Westminster, the National Members, being free of English Party whips, will certainly be able to enforce attention to Scottish affairs to a much greater degree than is possible by Party Members dominated and controlled by huge English Majorities within these parties, whose policies are formulated in accordance with the entirely different or varying conditions appertaining to England. Every possible effort will be made by National Members to bring to the forefront all Scottish matters and interests.

FREEDOM   JUSTICE   PROGRESS

VOTE NATIONALIST

WORK FOR SCOTLAND   JOIN THE NATIONAL PARTY

standing for the Reconstruction of Scottish National Life, including Self-Government for Scotland with Independent

NATIONAL STATUS WITHIN THE BRITISH GROUP OF NATIONS

Read the "SCOTS INDEPENDENT." 2d. Monthly.

Printed by Robert Thomson, 11 Spoutmouth, Glasgow, C.1.
Published by National Party of Scotland, 131 West Regent Street, Glasgow, C.2.
Leaflet No. 11 (6/5/29)

The National Party of Scotland At Westminster campaign leaflet, 1929

John MacCormick at the time of founding SNP, 1934

R. E. Muirhead, standing, profile, John MacCormick leaning over table,
R. B. Cunninghame Graham signing a resolution, 1930

Covenant National Committee, circa 1950: (back row left to right)
——, J. M. Rollo, ——, Sir John Cameron K C, Michael Byrne, ——, ——,
Nigel Tranter,—— (Andrew Haddon is in the back row, one or other side of
Nigel Tranter), ——, John Bayne, Robin Orr, J. J. Campbell
(front row left to right), Dr John MacDonald, W. Ross Maclean QC, William
Power, John MacCormick, Robert Gray, Professor A. Dewar Gibb, ——

John MacCormick canvassing support for the Scottish Convention, late 1940s

John MacCormick playing toy soldiers with sons Neil (centre) and Iain (rhs)

John MacCormick addressing a Scottish Convention Meeting,
St Andrew's Hall, Glasgow 1949

The Flag in the Wind on sale, 1955!

John MacCormick as Rector of Glasgow University, 1951

The author's son, Neil MacCormick

One by one the leaders of the two factions put their case, while I sat silent wondering what the outcome might be. At last it came the turn of Angus Clark to speak in his own defence. Never have I heard a more eloquent or restrainedly impassioned statement. He was a native Gaelic speaker bred in Ballachulish and, in spite of many years in London, his voice still carried a strong Highland inflection which like some nostalgic music stirred me strangely. Nearly everything he said appealed strongly to the more romantic side of my nature. He was out and out for Scotland's independent nationhood and no compromise. Those who sought for practical means of attaining even a tithe of what he wanted were mere timeservers, careerists, traitors to the cause. With a scornful gesture he pointed to me as a young upstart who would soon find his proper place in English politics. "Let us," he said, "take a leaf from the pages of Ireland's recent history, and let us remember our own more ancient past."

He ended by quoting that memorable phrase from the Declaration of Arbroath:

"For as long as one hundred of us remain alive we shall never submit to the dominion of the English."

When he sat down there was a tremendous outburst of applause from the whole assembly. Every member there was visibly moved by his impassioned sincerity and obvious good faith. I felt that the day was lost and I almost rose to move that the resolutions should be withdrawn. Instead I replied with as much coolness as I could to his charges of treachery and careerism. We in this hall, I suggested, were not the Scottish nation, however much we might be tempted so to picture ourselves. The nation was not an abstraction, an imaginary Dark Rosaleen, but a living reality composed of millions of living individual people. It was with the people we had to contend and it was their mood which we must seek to interpret. We could only be effective leaders of opinion so long as we did not race too far ahead of those whom we wished to follow us.

I think Angus Clark's eloquence was in a sense his own undoing for it had keyed me up to a similar pitch. Slowly but surely I felt that the audience was beginning to be impressed by my argument, and the more I felt it the more strongly did I dare to speak. I cannot now remember all that I said but it is still vividly in my mind that when I sat down after fifteen minutes I felt utterly exhausted, as though I had drained myself of every ounce of nervous energy. It was only dimly that I heard the swelling applause and the countering shouts of disapproval.

There were loud calls to the Chairman to take the vote without further debate and he had no choice but to yield to the clamour. The alternatives were put to the meeting and by a considerable majority the expulsion resolutions were carried. I had no feeling of triumph. I was sorry to part with such men as Angus Clark and in the reaction to excitement I could not but ask myself whether, after all, such drastic measures had been necessary. It was with a dry mouth and a heavy heart that I made my way from the meeting despite the handshakes and back-slapping congratulations of dozens of supporters.

Nevertheless, it was soon apparent that by the decisions then taken we had enabled ourselves to seize a new opportunity.

The Kilmarnock Burghs constituency in Ayrshire had fallen vacant and we had intimated to the Press that our candidate would be John M. McNicol. Almost simultaneously the Scottish Party announced their intention of putting forward a candidate and they nominated Professor Dewar Gibb. We would, therefore, have been faced with the ludicrous situation in which two candidates standing for almost identical objectives would have been competing for public support.

We now, however, felt that our hands were free for negotiation with the Scottish Party and on our invitation a joint meeting was held before nomination day in Kilmarnock.

Without much difficulty the representatives of the two organisations were able to reach agreement on the following joint statement:

"As both Parties firmly believe in the right of the Scottish people to determine the future status of Scotland it has been found possible to agree upon a joint candidate going forward with the following aim:

"The establishment in Scotland of a Parliament which shall be the final authority on all Scottish affairs including taxation and finance.

"Both parties are agreed that the institution of tariff barriers between England and Scotland is undesirable and that Imperial matters defence and foreign policy should remain matters of joint concern between Scotland and England. There shall only be such future modification or revision of the Act of Union as is necessary to obtain the foregoing objects."

There remained only the selection of a suitable candidate to represent the united front. Both McNicol and Gibb readily agreed to stand down so as to facilitate our choice, and, thereafter, Sir Alexander MacEwen was unanimously selected.

The by-election which followed was fought intensively over a period of only three weeks. Sir Alexander put up a magnificent fight and the two parties co-operated without a hitch. Although time was against us and we still had to overcome the drop in our influence which had followed the fiasco in East Fife we succeeded in completely recovering all our lost ground. Sir Alexander polled over 6,000 votes and pushed our percentage up to 17, the highest yet recorded for a Nationalist candidate. Once again we had demonstrated that even temporary setbacks could not arrest our steady progress and that the day might soon come when Nationalist candidates would hold the balance of power in Scotland.

We had, moreover, made it certain that the two Home Rule parties would unite, and after the usual procedure of joint discussions and references back to delegate conferences, complete agreement was achieved and the parties were merged, under the name of the Scottish National Party, in April, 1934.

I well remember the final meeting of the joint negotiating committee when we gathered to celebrate the success of our endeavours. Cunninghame Graham, who had throughout encouraged us in the policies which we had followed, entertained us all to dinner in the Central Hotel. We felt that we had taken a real step forward in the fight for a new Scotland and our mood was one both of gaiety and of an underlying realisation of the opportunities which now opened before us. In one of those gestures which he so loved and always carried off so well Cunninghame Graham suddenly called for champagne all round and rose to drink a toast to the future. With a profound bow to the Duke of Montrose he acknowledged him as the head of the clan and then went on to say:

"Gentlemen, this is an occasion in the history of Scotland and it would be a strange thing if there were not at least two Grahams present. The name which I share with His Grace has played its part in the making of our history since the dimmest ages of the past. Does not legend have it that the very first barbarous and probably naked Scot who breached Antonine's Roman Wall was one called Graham and, thereafter, that rampart of the world's mightiest Empire was known contemptuously to our countrymen as Graham's Dyke. Perhaps we have breached another wall today, or perhaps we are only gathering the forces that will yet do so. I give you the toast of Scotland and who better is there to reply than the chief of the Clan Graham."

CHAPTER FOURTEEN

THE HOPES WHICH had been aroused by the fusion of the two parties were destined to be postponed by events over which no one in Scotland had any control. Hitler had come to power in Germany in 1933 and the excesses of his propaganda gave to the very word "nationalism" a new and highly distasteful meaning. It was in vain for us to point out that nationalism in Scotland had a very different meaning from the nationalism of the Nazi Party. The ordinary man found it difficult to draw any such distinction and gradually there began to attach to us something of the odium which rightly belonged to the Fascist and National Socialist movements. The irony of such a situation lay in the fact that it would be difficult to imagine any group of people in the world less likely to succumb to totalitarian ideas than the people who led the National Movement in Scotland or to think of any nation to which such ideas were more alien than Scotland.

For my own part, as time went on I found myself increasingly willing to take part in those movements of a "united front" against Fascism which were so much a feature of Radical politics in the late 'thirties. I detested the compromises of Munich and was almost willing to forget my Scottish nationalism in my hatred of the cruel thing which racialism had become. These developments, however, took place gradually over the years and, at first, the new Scottish National Party seemed well set for steady forward progress. By the time the General Election of 1935 arrived we had considerably strengthened our organisation and were able to put forward twelve candidates instead of the mere five with which we had to be content in 1931.

Among the seats which we now contested were the Scottish Universities with Professor Gibb as our candidate and the Western Isles with Sir Alexander MacEwen. In each of these constituencies we did extremely well, gaining over 25 per cent. of the poll and in Inverness-shire, which I contested again our percentage rose from 14 per cent. to 16 per cent. Unfortunately, however, in the other constituencies we fared badly and, even where we had previously done reasonably well, such as in Dunbartonshire and East Renfrewshire, our poll dropped and the deposit was lost.

There were, of course, good reasons for our failure. The Labour Party, which had fared so badly in 1931, made an all-out effort to recover its lost ground and, wherever Nationalist candidates appeared, was loud in its promises of Scottish Home Rule. The Government Coalition, on the other hand, proclaimed that its policy was to strengthen the League of Nations and to maintain peace through collective security. So widespread was the fear of war and so alarming were the threats of aggression from Japan, Italy and Germany that the majority of electors, in Scotland as in England, were completely hoodwinked by the Government's peace pledges and returned the Coalition with a reduced but still very substantial majority. It was foreseen by no one that first in Manchuria then in Abyssinia and finally in Czechoslovakia the Government which was pledged to collective security would betray its own promises and by its weakness make war inevitable.

The Liberal Party, which under Sir Herbert Samuel and Sir Archibald Sinclair had broken away from the national Coalition, fared little better than the Scottish National Party and its already small numbers in Parliament dropped to a mere handful. None the less it still held a few Scottish constituencies and since, prior to the General Election campaign, Sir Herbert Samuel had renewed the Liberal pledges on

Home Rule, it began to seem to many Nationalists that in the future we might make common cause with the Liberal Party.

In the House of Commons from 1935 to 1939, Sir Archibald Sinclair, despite the smallness of his following, played a leading part in opposition to the Government's vacillating and pusillanimous foreign policy and, in many ways, he seemed to be an excellent spokesman for enlightened Scottish opinion. While he had always paid lip-service to the Liberal policy of Scottish Home Rule he had, I thought, been rather lukewarm about it, but it now seemed that at least he should be approached to discover whether there was any possibility of a working arrangement.

Accordingly, with the full knowledge and consent of such leading members of the National Party as the Duke of Montrose, Sir Alexander MacEwen and Professor Gibb, but without any formal authorisation by our National Council, I communicated with the Scottish Liberal Federation through Lady Louise Glen-Coats who was its most active member.

I found that she was genuinely enthusiastic on the Home Rule issue and that in most matters she held views very similar to my own. She was by no means averse to the idea that our two parties might collaborate and, in due course, early in 1937, she invited me to Hollybush House in Ayrshire, which was then her home, for a private meeting with Sir Archibald Sinclair and Sir Robert Hamilton who, until he had lost his seat in Parliament, had been Chief Liberal Whip and who was still a leading adviser of the Parliamentary Liberal Party.

My appointment with them was for dinner at seven o'clock and I left my office in Glasgow in what I thought was good time to motor down to Hollybush. My car, however, was of very ancient vintage and, unfortunately, before I reached Ayr one of my rear tyres blew out. At the best of times I was always a somewhat improvident motorist and on this occasion I was carrying no jack. Having often before had to deal with similar emergencies I drove the wheel on to the grass verge, propped the axle up with stones and proceeded to dig a hole under the offending tyre with no better tools than a spanner and the starting handle. With much labour and at the cost of a good deal of perspiration I managed at last to make a deep enough cavity to allow the wheel to slip off its bolts.

The whole operation of changing the wheel took more than half an hour and considering that my spare was already badly blistered it was with feelings of some uneasiness that I now tried to hurry to make up for lost time. Fortune favoured me, however, and without further mishap I arrived at Hollybush grimy and dishevelled but less than half an hour late.

I confess that I was a little bit taken aback when I saw the size of the establishment. Lady Glen-Coats' husband, Sir Thomas, was one of the Coats of Paisley and while I knew he must be a very wealthy man I had not reflected that he would probably live in considerable style. As I drew up at the large door I became acutely conscious of the battered and weatherbeaten appearance of my old car and of the grime which I had collected on my own person when changing the wheel. To my further consternation it was actually a butler who received me and who seemed to look me up and down with the supercilious hauteur which only such a dignitary can command.

I gave my name. "Oh yes, sir," he said, "her Ladyship's expecting you. They've just started dinner and I'll show you in whenever you're ready. Would you like a wash?" The question was so obviously superfluous that I smiled wanly and muttered something about having had trouble with my car.

"Ah yes, yes," he said smoothly with a glance in the direction of my old wreck, "even the most dependable of them let us down sometimes. Just come this way, sir."

I washed as quickly and thoroughly as I could and presented myself again to the care of the butler in the hall. He swung open the door of the dining-room with a flourish and announced me, "Mr. John MacCormick, Your Ladyship."

It was a large and lovely room and, at what seemed to me to be an immense distance away, the dinner party was seated around a long and beautifully polished table. To my further consternation the gentlemen were immaculate in dinner jackets and Lady Glen-Coats was wearing a shimmering silver-grey evening gown. I was in a shabby office suit from which I had only been able partially to brush the considerable quantity of good Ayrshire soil which had accumulated upon it.

Never in my life had I felt more nervous and embarrassed nor more unworthy of what should have been an important occasion. I was, of course, received by Lady Glen-Coats and Sir Thomas with perfect hospitality and after introductions to the guests I made what shift I could to answer reasonably the usual polite questions about my journey. I was seated at one end of the long table beside Sir Thomas and opposite Sir Archibald Sinclair and, since I declined any preliminaries, the main course was almost immediately placed before me. It consisted of two grilled chops served with those small green peas which always seem more completely spherical than any others. As I raised the first forkful to my mouth luck would have it that one of them fell off, audibly bounced on the polished mahogany and rolled the whole length of the table towards my hostess, leaving as it went a faint but very visible greasy track. I gazed at it in a final horror of discomfiture!

Not until coffee and liqueurs were being served did I begin
to recover my composure and to take any really conscious
part in the conversation. But I shall always be grateful to
Lady Glen-Coats for the skill with which she covered up my
embarrassment and gradually succeeded in drawing me out
so that finally I was completely at ease. The evening, indeed,
proved very successful as well as enjoyable and I found that
both the Liberal leaders were genuinely interested in the
possibility of some kind of working arrangement with the
Scottish National Party. Our talk, of course, was entirely
informal and noncommittal but I sensed that, despite my
bad beginning I was making at least a partially favourable
impression on Sir Archibald and his friend. That feeling was
confirmed when, after I had indicated that it was time for
me to take the road back to Glasgow, I was cordially pressed
to continue the conversation one evening in the following
week. Sir Archibald and Sir Robert were proceeding next
morning to spend a few days in Caithness and it was arranged
that on their return they would again break their journey at
Hollybush for a further meeting.

On the occasion of this second visit I took adequate precautions. I borrowed a fine black limousine from a more
affluent friend and in the late afternoon changed hurriedly
in my office into dinner dress. In due course I arrived at
Hollybush absolutely up to time and feeling quite irreproach-
able, having stopped at a local hotel for a final wash and
brush-up, and for a modest helping of Dutch courage. Again
I was ushered in to the company by the butler who I thought
this time looked at me with the hint of a smile in his eyes.
In a moment I knew why. Out of respect to my appearance
in the previous week, they were now all dressed in what
looked to be the roughest tweeds and oldest flannels in their
wardrobes!

For an instant I felt again like a fish out of water but Sir

Archibald laughed. "You've turned the tables on us this time!" he exclaimed, and, thus, the ice was completely broken. With a glass of sherry in my hand I confessed how embarrassed I had been at our first meeting and the whole story of my journey and arrival and of my subterfuges of tonight made a good beginning to our meal.

Later in the evening we reached a tentative agreement. At the next General Election, which, at that time, was expected within a year, the Scottish National Party would contest twelve seats of their own choosing and the Liberal Party would avoid putting up candidates against us. They would, moreover, put whatever local organisation they had at our disposal and would publicly recommend their followers to support us. We were asked to make no commitment in return other than to restrict ourselves to twelve seats, which, in any case, I knew privately would strain our small resources to their utmost.

We further discussed the possibility of issuing something in the nature of a joint manifesto on Scottish self-government but we agreed to leave that project over to a later occasion. I arranged that on Sir Archibald's next return to Scotland I should meet him again and would have with me another of my colleagues so that what was now informally agreed could later be made official. He recalled that Dewar Gibb had served along with him during the war when they had both been young officers in Winston Churchill's regiment and said he would like to meet him again if I could arrange it. I promised to do so and we parted on the friendliest of terms.

I returned that night to Glasgow feeling that I had done some good work for the National Party and deeply grateful to Lady Glen-Coats for having acted as so excellent a mediator.

CHAPTER FIFTEEN

No opportunity presented itself for a further meeting with Sir Archibald Sinclair until well on in 1938, and, by that time, the gathering crisis in Europe had become so ominous that all men's minds were filled by it. We did, however, meet in the middle of that year, again in Holly-bush, and Dewar Gibb came with me to renew his old acquaintanceship and to stamp our talks with his authority, for he was now Chairman of the Scottish National Party. The arrangements which I had tentatively made a year before were confirmed and we even came around to the discussion of the terms of a joint declaration. Yet on both sides there was a feeling of unreality in our proposals. It was by now evident that a General Election might be indefinitely postponed and no one knew in what dire circumstances it might be fought. Sir Archibald Sinclair himself was deeply involved in the Parliamentary struggle to put backbone into British policy and often his was the only voice to echo Winston Churchill's warnings. He was obviously much preoccupied as we talked with him and I could see that in his eyes reform in the government of Scotland was a very minor matter as compared with the issues then confronting the world. I had no thought that come what may we should give up the struggle for Home Rule but I could not help understanding Sinclair's attitude. Dewar Gibb, I believe, was somewhat more impatient with him, but he, too, realised that events might well overturn any agreement we could make.

Within a month or two of that meeting Neville Chamberlain had signed the Munich Agreement and, to all who had eyes to see, war had been made inevitable. While I continued to maintain close and friendly contact with the Scottish Liberal Federation through Lady Glen-Coats it was obvious that circumstances would vastly alter the environment in which any arrangement between us could take effect.

The impact of the rapidly deteriorating world situation was, of course, felt strongly even within the ranks of our own Scottish National Party. Once again, a real and fundamental cleavage both of sentiment and opinion began to make itself evident. Conscription for military service had been introduced by the Government and many Nationalists urged that we should oppose any such measure to the point of civil disobedience and conscientious objection. They argued that Scotland was an unwilling partner in the Union and that no Scot could be compelled to serve in any army but by a Scottish government.

I could not see the force of such an argument. However unwillingly the ordinary people of Scotland had accepted the Union in 1707 they had undoubtedly acquiesced in it, to say the least, ever since. We in the National Party were still a minority in Scotland however widespread some degree of sympathy with us might be and we had no shadow of a right to claim that we spoke for the nation. It was, moreover, obvious that in no modern world war could even a completely independent Scotland remain neutral when England was involved. The facts of geography as well as of history compelled us to accept the necessity for a common policy both in defence and in international affairs. We had the right, like any other opposition party, to criticise the Government of the day but we had no right to contract out of obligations which were the burden of our common citizenship. In any case, the temper of our own people was strongly opposed to Nazism and Fascism and if the Scottish National Party were to take any stand which laid us open to the charge of being lukewarm in the cause of European freedom we should lose all chance of increasing our strength.

This attitude commanded the support of a clear majority of our members but the malcontents were noisy and troublesome. An association called the Scottish Neutrality League was formed among them and their activities cost us, as I thought, much loss of support among the public.

At first, however, what I regarded as the sane element in the Party kept the situation well in hand and we were able to march in step with Scottish public opinion. When finally war broke out we adopted a strongly worded resolution pledging full support to the war effort although reserving the right to speak out for what we believed were Scotland's special interests. We recognised that the impact of war would inevitably restrict our capacity for propaganda but we were determined to maintain the identity of our movement.

There were, indeed, many matters connected with the war effort in which it was necessary for us to speak our minds. The arrangements for defence against air attack were far from satisfactory, there being no fighter command situated in Scotland. Despite the rapid growth of the armaments industry there were still idle factories in Scotland used only for storage and thousands of Scottish girls were being drafted compulsorily for war work in England. In these and other similar respects there was continuing need for a National Party capable always of voicing a purely Scottish point of view.

In 1940, an opportunity came our way to call attention vividly to our protests. The constituency of Argyll had fallen vacant through the death of F. A. McQuiston, and since the major parties had agreed upon a political truce it was expected that whoever might be chosen by the Unionists to succeed him would be returned unopposed.

But the Scottish National Party was under no obligation

to observe the truce and with little hesitation we decided to put forward a candidate. In all the circumstances, however, we knew that it was essential to choose someone who was widely respected and who could not be accused of even the slightest disloyalty to the war effort.

Fortunately, we had such a person readily to hand. He was William Power, who, ever since his retiral from the Editorship of the *Scots Observer* some years before, had taken an active part in all our work and was now our Vice-Chairman. He was, in quite a unique sense, the doyen of Scottish journalism and was universally loved and admired. He had written so much and for so many years in the popular Press that his name was a household word and although his nationalism was profound and sincere no one could suppose for a moment that he would countenance any folly of extremism. The only difficulty was that he was now sixty-nine years of age and Argyll was so extensive and scattered a constituency that we hesitated to ask him to undertake such a strenuous campaign.

When finally it was put to him, however, he agreed willingly and complained only that he was completely un-accustomed to electioneering and might disappoint us on the platform. These objections were quickly waved aside and very soon we found ourselves once again in the throes of a by-election and in a constituency where we had no semblance of organisation whatever.

Despite that handicap it soon became obvious that we were gathering support from all quarters except among the die-hard Tories. It was the first time that we had ever engaged in a straight fight and it was very illuminating to learn from hundreds of staunch Labour and Liberal Party supporters that they had only been awaiting such an opportunity to vote outright for Home Rule without thereby denying party loyalty. William Power himself rose magnificently to the occasion and travelled tirelessly over the whole wide area and even to the scattered islands of the Inner Hebrides. So great was the obvious popular response to his appeal that a few days before polling day it was being freely forecast on all hands and even in the daily Press that he would win. In places as widely separated as Dunoon and Campbeltown and Oban packed meetings were cheering us to the echo when the Tory candidate, Major Duncan McCallum, could hardly gather any audience at all.

But once again the fates were against us. Our fortunes had risen in the hot-house atmosphere of the "phoney" war at a time when it seemed little trouble to "hang out the washing on the Siegfried Line". Then, twenty-four hours before the opening of the poll in Argyll, there came the dread news that the war had become a reality at last. Hitler had loosed his armies upon Norway, Denmark and Holland defying their neutrality and thus proclaiming the full depth of his intent. On the morning after the news had broken it seemed that every newspaper in the country directed its attention to Argyll. To vote for the Government was now declared to be a sacred duty and to vote against it to be a display of cowardly weakness in the face of the aggressor. We, who had fought so hard and overcome so many obstacles in our fight for Scotland, now knew only too well what would happen on election day.

In the event our worst fears were far from being realised. William Power polled 8,000 votes against the Government's 12,000 in spite of the official and loudly announced condemnation of us by every other party in the State. It was clear that even in the dark threat of war the slowly awakening spirit of Scotland could not be quenched. Having already in advance accepted failure we were at the end of the day elated by the result and the handful of speakers who had covered nearly all the ancient kingdom of Dalriada gathered not by plan but by instinct in the Stag Hotel, Lochgilphead, to celebrate another battle and to talk of the next advance. It was only then that William Power showed any sign of fatigue. In the last three weeks he had travelled thousands of miles and spoken at hundreds of meetings. Never once had he taken a wrong step or given opportunity to those who sought with eagle eye to see us in a snare. He had been the perfect candidate, uniting under his banner all the diverse elements who fought for Scotland. Even Angus Clark, who, seven years before, had been expelled, returned to the fold and speaking in the ancient language of the country won much support among those older voters whose racial memory was more potent than any newfangled politics.

But on this night, after the declaration of the poll, William Power alone among us was depressed and aware of defeat. His feelings were the product of utter exhaustion and were deepened by the modesty which was so natural to him and which made him feel that somehow he had been personally inadequate as our standard-bearer. I had a strong affection for him and on a sudden impulse I told him something which a kind of shyness had prevented me ever saying before.

Many years ago, at the age of sixteen, I had been an office-boy to a firm of lawyers in Glasgow. One of my daily duties was to walk from St. Vincent Street to the Sheriff Court with various documents for lodgement, and I usually chose a roundabout route which took me through St. George's Place where one of the biggest bookshops in Glasgow had its premises. I could there browse among the capacious shelves almost unnoticed and in five-minute instalments on my outward and return journeys I contrived to skim through most of the books which took my fancy.

One book which had recently been published by a little-known local publisher and whose author was quite unknown to me demanded more than mere skimming. It was a volume

of essays written with distinctly Scottish inspiration called
The World Unvisited. I was completely fascinated by it and
longed to have it for more careful reading among my own
small possession of books. But it was priced at 8*s*. 6*d*. which
was far beyond my means, and I knew I would have to be
content with moments snatched from time.

Having broken myself away from it reluctantly one
morning I proceeded on my way and reached the Process
Room in the Sheriff Court Buildings. The clerk behind the
counter was patiently but almost unavailingly explaining to
a down-and-out Jew, whose English was very imperfect,
that, if he wished to defend an action which had been raised
against him, he must first state his case in writing. When the
clerk saw me he called me over to him and in a whisper
described the Jew's predicament.

"For heaven's sake," he said, "take him into a corner, get
his story and write out his defence. Charge him ten bob and
no one will be any wiser!"

Willingly I did as I was told. My modest (and quite illicit)
fee was paid without protest and within ten minutes I was the
proud possessor of a copy of *The World Unvisited* by William
Power. That was how I spent the first legal fee I ever earned,
little dreaming that a day would come when the same
William Power would be one of my closest friends and
colleagues.

My recital of that story late at night in the heart of mid-
Argyll seemed to act like a tonic on Power. His depression
disappeared and a new feeling of confidence emanated from
him. I think he must suddenly have realised that the many
material rewards which he had so often spurned were well
enough replaced by the affection in which a younger Scottish
generation held him.

CHAPTER SIXTEEN

An immediate, but very temporary, result of the Argyll election was the closing of our ranks in the National Party. For the moment the differences among us were forgotten and at our Annual Conference which was held shortly afterwards William Power was unanimously elected Chairman of the Party. It looked as though we had convinced even the most intransigent of our followers that the path of moderation was the one most likely to gain the support of our countrymen.

My own experience as Power's election agent in Argyll, involving as it did many conversations with leading local Labourites, Liberals and even dissident Unionists in my search for support, induced in me a new train of thought. It was obvious that many of these people were as eager to obtain a measure of Scottish Home Rule as we were ourselves but, in ordinary circumstances, the habits of party loyalty made it difficult, if not impossible, for them to vote for Nationalist candidates. The political truce would not last for ever and we should seldom have another opportunity for a straight fight. Was it not possible, therefore, to adopt some new tactic which would enable us effectively to enlist the support of members of all parties instead of frightening them off by challenging their candidates at the polls?

I allowed such ideas meantime to simmer in my mind but very soon the neutralists in our ranks began to raise their voices again and to cause trouble at all our Party meetings. Owing to the natural draining away of many of our best people to the Forces the relative strength of what had been a small minority among us was growing, and it became increasingly clear to me and my immediate associates that sooner or later there would have to be a show-down and if necessary a complete break.

The disaffected element in the Party had now obtained a leader capable of wielding considerable influence. He was Douglas Young, then a lecturer in Greek in Aberdeen University, and a very striking figure indeed. He was over 6 feet 5 inches in height and wore a neatly trimmed black beard. He was forceful and eloquent in public speech and a most persuasive talker in private conversation. He had joined the Party some years ago but, except in Aberdeen, he had not made any great impact on the movement until now.

By refusing to accept his call-up notice to the Forces, however, he now leapt into prominence. He pleaded before the Conscientious Objectors' Tribunal not that he was a pacifist, but that, as a Scotsman, no Government of the United Kingdom had power to impose conscription upon him. He quoted the terms of the Treaty of Union in support of his case but, needless to say, the Tribunal rejected his plea. When he then indicated that he would, in any case, refuse call-up and suffer imprisonment rather than yield, he became the hero and the natural leader of the anti-war section of the National Party. Matters came to a head when, after having been sentenced in the Sheriff Court to one year's imprisonment and while still awaiting his appeal to the High Court, he was nominated for the Chairmanship of the Party in opposition to William Power at our Annual Conference in June, 1942.

Prior to the Conference I had placed a resolution on the agenda to the effect that the Party, having served its pioneering purpose by fighting elections against all other parties should now regard itself as the agency which might unite Scottish opinion, irrespective of party differences, behind an agreed measure of Scottish Home Rule. In putting such a

resolution forward I knew that it would be strongly opposed
by the extreme element but all my friends agreed that it was
essential to try to make use of the growing sympathy towards
our point of view, which was, at this time, manifesting itself
on all hands and even in Parliament. Tom Johnston was
now Secretary of State in Churchill's Cabinet and, largely
through his influence, a new and constructive spirit of
co-operation on matters affecting Scotland was developing
among the parties. In any case, we felt that the division in
our ranks was now creating such a strain upon us all that it
was better to face up to a final trial of strength than to waste
more time on makeshift compromises.

The Conference in 1942 was held in the Shandwick
Galleries on a very hot Saturday in June. In spite of the
depletion in our numbers through war service there was a
large attendance of delegates and one could sense the strained
atmosphere from the very beginning of the proceedings.

The first row developed early in the formal business when
Dr. John Macdonald was presenting his report as Editor of
our journal, *The Scots Independent*. He had been one of my
closest associates ever since 1929, and had rendered invaluable services to the Party as speaker, organiser and Editor of
our publications. Everyone knew that he had been tireless
in the cause and that he had always tried to hold an even
balance among the varied points of view within the movement. I was, therefore, astonished when he was almost
shouted down as he proceeded with his report. His offence
had been the publication of an article mildly critical of
Douglas Young's objections to war service! And the people
who were howling at him were nearly all very recent
members of the Party who had performed no service for it
except to disturb its meetings. It was at once obvious that the
opposition to the Executive had been strongly organised and
that every delegate upon whom the supporters of Young

could lay their hands had been dragged out to the Conference.

After much heated discussion Dr. Macdonald's report was at last approved by a very narrow majority. Then came the election of office-bearers with, of course, the crucial decision to be made at the very beginning as to whether William Power or Douglas Young should be Chairman of the Party. The two contestants retired, our Vice-Chairman, J. M. McNicol, took the chair and proposers and seconders were called for to speak on behalf of their nominees. As one of the proposers I spoke for Power but most of my ten minutes' speech was quite inaudible so great was the uproar. For the first time ever on a platform I felt anger rising within me, and bitterness as well. William Power had served us faith-fully and well for years and even long before the formation of the National Party he had done much through his writings to create a new interest in things Scottish. Yet here, where he should have been the most honoured among us all, his sponsors could hardly make themselves heard!

I tried to keep the anger out of my voice but when I sat down again I had made up my mind. Whichever way the vote might go there must be a parting of the ways for the two sections in the Party. I could not even try to listen to the remaining speeches, so strongly did I feel the affront to Power. When the vote came I was almost relieved—William Power was defeated by two votes! McNicol from the Chair called for a recount which was no more than reasonable but he was shouted down. I leaned over and whispered to him.

"Let it be," I said. "I wouldn't now insult William Power by asking him to be the Chairman of this rabble." McNicol seemed to agree with me and there and then declared Douglas Young elected.

As was customary the new Chairman, loudly applauded by his supporters, was now brought back to the hall and installed in the Chair. He was obviously elated and excited and he turned to me as Honorary Secretary for guidance as to the next business. I said I would like to address the meeting briefly and he called upon me, not guessing what I was about to say.

In as few words as possible I told the delegates that I was disgusted by the proceedings and that I believed people who conducted themselves in such a manner would never achieve anything, let alone self-government for Scotland.

I had no feeling of rancour against Douglas Young whom they had just elected and who, I was certain, would as deeply regret any personal attack on William Power as I did myself. But, in his election, decisions had been taken on matters of principle which far transcended personalities and, in effect, the Party had gone back on its former resolution to give full support to the war effort. Although I was nominated as National Secretary, and, indeed, had been the only person nominated ever since 1929, I now felt I had no alternative but to decline the office and intimate my resignation from the Party. As I spoke I was listened to this time in silence, for I think no one in the opposition had fully realised what their outcry must lead to. When I finished there was a moment's pause, then one by one delegate after delegate rose to say that he also wished to resign. I was astonished, and, although my heart was heavy at the thought of leaving the Party which I had done so much to create and build up, I was also pleased to see one after another nearly all the former office-bearers and the men and women who had done the real spade-work for Nationalism follow my example.

William Power himself was in a dilemma and I could see that he was hesitating as to what to do. Being the defeated candidate he could not act out of what might seem to be mere personal umbrage, which, I am sure, he never felt.

Suddenly, however, he found his own way out of his difficulty.

"Mr. Chairman," he said, "I congratulate you on your election, I bear you no ill-will and, while I do not agree with the position you have taken up about war service, I admire your courage in defying popular opinion. But it seems to me that a decision has been taken not on persons but on a principle. I, therefore, will go with John MacCormick. I, too, resign."

His statement was greeted almost equally by applause and jeers. But it left me in no further doubt what to do. I had already left the platform and now I stood up at the back of the hall and, shouting above the din, invited all those who had resigned to cross the road to the Rutland Hotel where future action could be considered. There was an immediate move towards the door by thirty or forty of the delegates and I walked out. Thus, after fourteen years of endeavour in which I had spent nearly all my energies in the service of the National Party, my connection with it came suddenly to an end.

CHAPTER SEVENTEEN

ALTHOUGH THE EVENTS which led up to the breakaway
from the Scottish National Party appeared to be confused
by personal issues and although the impact of the war
against Hitlerism was the immediate cause of differences
among us, the disruption was, in fact, the culmination of
many years of internal argument and strife in the Nationalist
Movement. Naturally, I cannot claim impartiality in my
judgement since I was centrally involved in all these disputes,
but, as I now look back, I am convinced that the split was
inevitable and that if we had sought any longer to patch up
our differences the result would have been to thwart us all,
on both sides of the fence, in our endeavours. It seemed to
me then, and events have since largely justified my opinion,
that what I called the wild men in the party were by nature
intolerant, not only of my friends and myself, but of each
other as well. As individuals they were no doubt excellent
people who held sincerely and courageously to their opinions,
but each was a party in himself and all lacked the power to
cohere in a common cause. The very word "compromise"
was anathema to them, yet compromise, up to a proper
limit, is the essence of all successful political endeavour.
They belonged to a type which has always played a significant and even a valuable part in the life of Scotland but it
seemed to me that, in the circumstances of modern life, they
were too rigid in their logic to be effective as a fighting
force. In the twelve years that have followed our walk-out
there have been many more disputes within the National
Party and it is surely significant that Douglas Young, R. E.
Muirhead, Dr. Lamont, Oliver Brown and many other of

the leading personalities who then took over the guidance of the Party are now themselves no longer leaders of it. They have gone their several ways as they were always bound to do.

Among those who gathered in the Rutland Hotel on that summer afternoon in 1942, were nearly all the former leading office-bearers of the National Party, the men who in many years of self-sacrifice and ceaseless effort had brought it out of complete obscurity to a recognised place in the life of the country. They have all held together ever since and by their endeavours have made that small original band of seceders the largest and most influential Home Rule organisation which Scotland has ever known.

Our first task, of course, was to find a name for the new body which we then decided to form. After some deliberation we selected the title "Scottish Convention", thus using a word which had rich significance in Scottish constitutional history and which in its essential meaning implied the coming together of the community. We declared our aims to be twofold: first that we would seek to discover the highest common factor of national agreement on the reform of Scottish Government and would then bend our efforts towards achieving that reform; and second that we would try to examine Scottish economic and social problems from a non-party point of view, in the belief that many of them could be solved by almost unanimous national agreement. As a matter of policy we renounced the fighting of Parliamentary elections and held our ranks open to members of all parties or of none.

The public response to our declaration in these terms was immediate and substantial. Within a few weeks Scottish Convention could boast a membership of well over 1000 and very soon thereafter branches were successfully established in most parts of Scotland. It was, of course, impossible in time of war to conduct a really intensive campaign but what we succeeded in doing was to gather into our ranks a great many people who had always favoured some measure of Home Rule but who had looked either with suspicion or distaste at the activities of the National Party. Even a handful of members of Parliament joined us and spoke from our platform.

Indeed, at that time a new spirit seemed to have entered Scottish political life. The party truce had quenched the fires (always rather artificially maintained) of sectional dispute, and, under the leadership of Tom Johnston as Secretary of State in the Coalition Government, Scottish members of Parliament were learning to co-operate as a national group instead of dissipating their influence in wrangling among themselves.

In May, 1942, during a debate on Scottish Affairs in the House of Commons, many members of both parties expressed sentiments of strongly Nationalist flavour, and in a masterly survey of the years between the two wars Mr. Johnston showed that he was fully alive to the need for drastic reform. So much were the speeches to the point of all our propaganda that the very first publication to be issued by Scottish Convention was entitled *Hansard on Scotland* and contained a verbatim report of the Parliamentary debate.

In these years of necessarily reduced activity I found myself reassessing my own political opinions. Since I was no longer a member of the National Party, and Scottish Convention had renounced any idea of fighting elections, I was free to join any political party I chose. Naturally, my first consideration would be to do what might seem most likely to advance the cause of Scottish self-government but I could not in honesty identify myself with any party unless I could give general assent to its principles.

During all the time that my allegiance was given to the Scottish National Party I had vaguely regarded myself as a

Radical in the old Scottish sense of the word although, of course, I was associated with people of very varied political views, who were united only on the Scottish issue. It now at first seemed most appropriate that I should go back to the Labour Party which had in very large measure inherited the radicalism of the late nineteenth century. I knew that I would be welcomed there, for many times my old comrades of the I.L.P. had urged me both privately and in the Labour Press to return to the Labour fold where, they said, I would find far more opportunity of working for Scotland than I could in what they regarded as a hopeless wilderness.

Yet I hesitated to listen to their enticements. The Labour Party was by now a very different thing from the old free and easy I.L.P. It had already become a strictly disciplined machine and its leading thinkers seemed to be more and more fascinated by the idea of a rigidly planned economy in a centralised State. They had begun by looking with some-what uncritical awe at the boasted five-year plans of the Soviet Union and now their experience of wartime controls, when the State was effectively the only customer of industry, had confirmed them in the notion that Utopia could be constructed from a blue-print.

Both the rigid discipline of the Party and its growing faith in the panacea of planning, were distasteful to me. I could not picture myself jostling for advancement within an organisation in which credulous obedience to the party line was the surest road to success, nor could I believe that man's recipe for freedom and happiness was to be found in any pink re-hash of that horrible hotch-potch called Marxism-Leninism-Stalinism. Ideologies of any kind had always been anathema to me, and I had never believed that class politics could serve any valuable purpose for humanity. When, therefore, the final choice came and I was asked to accept Labour nomination as prospective candidate for

Inverness-shire just as Germany was beginning to collapse, I declined the invitation.

The Liberal Party at this time was well in its decline, but, for that very reason, it seemed that it might offer me an open platform on which I would be free to speak my mind both on political questions in general and on Scottish Home Rule in particular. It was the only party represented at Westminster which was fully pledged to support self-government and my own native radicalism would not run counter to such principles as it professed. Having first ascertained that there would be no serious objection to turning the Scottish Liberal Federation, which was an integral part of the British Liberal organisation, into an independent Scottish Liberal Party, I threw in my lot with the Liberals and bent myself to the task of helping to frame a new constitution for Liberalism in Scotland. In due course I was elected as Vice-Chairman of the Party and nominated as Liberal candidate for Inverness-shire in the General election of 1945. My election address on that occasion showed very little difference from those I had put forward on previous occasions as a Scottish Nationalist Candidate and despite the mortal wound which Liberalism then suffered throughout Great Britain the vote accorded to me for the same Scottish policies as I had propounded in 1935, showed an increase in numbers of over 2,000 and a rise in proportion of the poll from 16 per cent. to 25 per cent. It was enough to indicate to me that in spite of the interruption of war and the absence overseas of so many men of my own and younger generations, the Scottish Movement was still growing steadily and might soon be a power in the land.

My candidature then, of course, was not in any way sponsored by Scottish Convention which, as an all-party organisation, held itself entirely aloof from any electoral activity except to address a questionnaire on Home Rule to all the candidates in the Scottish constituencies. A majority of them responded well but we hesitated to place much faith in the promises of politicians who were eager to gather all the votes they could find.

The result of the election was, of course, an overwhelming victory for the Labour Party. By what amounted in England to a landslide the Tory Party was crushed and Mr. Attlee formed his first Government with the backing of a Parliamentary majority of something like 200. Strangely enough Scotland did not follow England's example and the representation from this country remained much as it was before polling took place. Even so, by a small margin Labour held the majority of Scottish seats and almost without exception every one of the Scottish Labour members had answered our Home Rule questions favourably. They now had the opportunity to give their promises effect!

Nor was it only the Scottish members who had made promises. In the election manifesto issued from Party Headquarters there appeared the slogan, "Labour believes in a Welsh Parliament for Welsh affairs, a Scottish Parliament for Scottish affairs, and a British Parliament for British affairs". As long ago as 1937 I had myself been present at a meeting in London, organised by a small group of Scottish Socialists who called themselves "The London Scots Self-Government Committee", at which no less a person than Mr. Attlee himself had solemnly and publicly pledged his Party to the policy of Home Rule for Scotland.

Events were soon to prove that Mr. Attlee had changed his mind and that the Labour Party of 1945 had very different ideas from those of its founders, James Keir Hardie and R. B. Cunninghame Graham.

CHAPTER EIGHTEEN

Now that Scottish Convention was set free from the restrictions of wartime we resumed our full-scale campaigning all over the country and wherever we went our meetings were well attended and new members in ever-increasing numbers were enrolled. It was clear that one of the effects of the war had been to heighten national consciousness in Scotland and, especially among the young men who were by now returning from the Forces, we found it easier than ever before to win converts to our cause. The deliberate moderation with which we stated our case and the fact that we demanded no sacrifice of party loyalties made our propaganda far more acceptable to the public than it had been in the days of our National Party membership and we became more and more assured that the drastic steps we had taken in 1942 were now being justified.

We were campaigning with a definite and immediate object in view. Our intention was to create enough public interest to enable us to bring together a fully representative conference which would discuss the future of Scotland and, if possible, agree on a minimum programme of demands. With a Labour Government in power and remembering all the promises which had been made, we hoped that if we could show widespread agreement on a measure of reform the Government would take appropriate action.

By the beginning of the year 1947 we were ready to put our plans into operation. On a close parallel to the old Conventions of Estates which had so often guided Scotland's destiny in moments of crisis in the past, we summoned a Scottish National Assembly to be held in Glasgow on 22nd

March that year. Invitations were sent to every local authority in the country, to the Presbyteries of the Church of Scotland, to trade unions, chambers of commerce, trade associations and every kind of public organisation. The result astonished even the most optimistic of us. Applications for delegate cards poured in from every corner of Scotland and when finally the Assembly met there were more than 600 delegates present representing so many local authorities and public bodies that we might claim with justice that this was a meeting which could speak for the whole nation. The *Scotsman* went so far as to describe the Assembly as the "most representative gathering of its kind ever brought together in Scotland".

It was the policy of Scottish Convention, having brought the Assembly together, to give the widest possible scope to the delegates in the discussion of Scotland's problem. We had, therefore, prepared an agenda consisting of a graded series of resolutions. The first expressed general satisfaction with the present set-up, the second demanded a number of fairly modest administrative reforms and the third requested the establishment of a Scottish Parliament within the framework of the United Kingdom.

We expected that each of these resolutions would obtain a fair amount of support and, although we naturally hoped that the third would win the majority, we took no active steps to influence the result. I had the honour of presiding over the meeting and I opened its proceedings by emphasising that we honestly desired to discover what, if any, measure of general agreement existed in Scotland.

Thereafter, to my own complete astonishment, one delegate after another rose to speak in favour of the third resolution. They came from every part of Scotland, from as far north as Shetland and as far south as Stranraer. They represented the Church, local authorities, trade unions and business associations, yet they spoke with one voice. Local grievances were recited from all corners of the country until, each added to the other, they became welded into a massive indictment of London control of Scottish affairs. There was no wrangling, none of that disputation to which the Scots are all too prone. Even the most irresponsible Nationalists, who had so often in the past turned meetings of the National Party into wild disorder, now put a curb on their tongues and spoke in sweetly reasonable tones! In the end, after a long discussion which was far more a demonstration of national unity than a debate, the third resolution, demanding a Scottish Parliament, was adopted with only two dissentient votes. There immediately followed such a spontaneous and prolonged outburst of applause that suddenly I knew with complete inward certainty that Scotland after so many years of sleep, had at last come back again to vigorous life. Ever since that moment I have never doubted that our objects will indeed be achieved, however long the road may be which we shall have to follow.

Having thus shown in the terms of a strongly worded but reasonable resolution that there existed in Scotland a very widespread degree of general agreement on the future of our nation, the Assembly proceeded to take the next practical step towards its goal. A Committee of the Assembly was appointed and charged with the task of preparing in complete detail a scheme for Scottish self-government which would give form and substance to the declaration contained in the resolution. The Committee was instructed to report back to a second Assembly within a year's time, and, in the meantime, when it had prepared its proposals, to seek an interview for discussion of them with the Prime Minister.

Since the business of the meeting was now concluded so satisfactorily I rose to thank the delegates for their forbearance with each other and with the Chairman and to declare the Assembly adjourned. But I had not completed my remarks when Professor Dewar Gibb stepped forward to the platform to interrupt me. Ever since the break-up of the Scottish National Party he had held aloof from Scottish Convention in the belief that I had acted rashly in endeavouring to launch a new organisation in the midst of all the difficulties of wartime. I had been distressed by apparently losing him for there was no one in Scotland with a keener brain and no one for whom I had more admiration and respect.

He now, to my surprise, called upon the meeting to show its thanks to me for having made such a demonstration of national unity possible. In terms which embarrassed me he spoke of my long service to the cause and for the second time that day the meeting broke spontaneously into prolonged applause. I was so completely taken off my guard that when finally I could make myself heard again I had great difficulty in controlling my voice, so deeply was I moved. I knew that what he praised me for had not been my doing but was simply the inevitable return to consciousness of a nation whose identity could never be destroyed, but, in the past, I had so often been the object of bitter personal attack that now I found it strange to receive so wholehearted a tribute. The importance of the occasion was to show how far we had all progressed from bitter partisanship towards real constructive unity of purpose.

The Committee appointed by the Assembly, consisting of some forty-five members was, in its own smaller compass, as representative as the Assembly itself. In approximately equal numbers it included members of the Tory and Labour Party, representatives of the Church, of local authorities and of various public bodies. It was the kind of committee which in Scotland might well have been expected to split hairs until Doomsday, but, instead, it was soon to show that when given some real hope for the future the Scots were no more unreasonably argumentative than their neighbours. It began its proceedings by appointing sub-committees—one to study the economic relations between England and Scotland, another to examine the legal and constitutional consequences of the establishment of a Scottish Parliament, a third to report upon the historical background and a fourth to consider the various forms of federal or near-federal government which had been successful in the modern world. Each group performed its task with care and thorough study, and, in the end, pooled the results of their research in general meeting. The outcome was that, within the year allotted to it, the full Committee of the Assembly was able, in complete unanimity, to prepare a detailed Scheme of Self-government for Scotland such as could, with very little adaptation, be transformed into an Act of the United Kingdom Parliament. The proposals thus prepared have since become widely known as "The Blue-Print for Scotland", and are included in this volume as Appendix One.

In the meantime, I had also been pursuing an alternative course of action. One or two of my most intimate colleagues had joined the Liberal Party along with me and two of them, Robert Gray and Dr. John Macdonald, were now, like myself, members of its Executive Committee. We were, therefore, in a position to negotiate with anyone who might come within negotiable distance, and suddenly, quite out of the blue, there appeared a star on the horizon. A young and vigorous Tory Member of Parliament, Peter Thorneycroft, had published, in conjunction with a few others of like mind a pamphlet under the title of *Design for Freedom*. It was an excellent, if somewhat woolly (and therefore self-contradictory) expression of the sentiments of what then remained of Liberalism in the modern world. It was clearly directed as a lover's dart at the now almost moribund Liberal Party, and

leading members of that organisation were invited to subscribe a statement approving of its proposals. I had already
been in touch with several Scottish Tory or National Liberal
Members of Parliament who were at least mildly affected by
the national awakening in Scotland and it seemed to me
that the *Design for Freedom* movement might create a bridge
over which they could march towards complete acceptance
of our national aims. I, therefore, subscribed the manifesto
which accompanied the pamphlet and my friends did likewise. Immediately thereafter we initiated a series of informal,
but almost authoritative conversations between representatives of the Scottish Liberal Party, the National Liberal Party
and the Scottish Unionist Party, in which leading members
of the Executive Committees of each organisation took part.

Finally, we reached the stage where the negotiators had
agreed on a draft joint statement of policy and it was intended
first to present the draft to our several executive committees
and then to full conferences of the parties. Had we been able
to carry out our programme and secure the agreement of the
three parties to our statement an entirely new political
situation would have arisen in Scotland. The three parties
would have merged and would quite certainly have been
able to command a majority of Parliamentary seats in
Scotland. The importance of the proceedings to me was that,
with the help of Robert Gray and John Macdonald as two
of my fellow representatives of the Liberal Party at the joint
meetings, I had been able to secure that the draft statement
included a fairly strong demand for devolution in the
government of Scotland. It was the first time that any leading
Unionists had agreed to press such a policy on their Party!

Unfortunately, events have a way of upsetting plans, and
what the negotiators hoped to achieve, and I think would
have achieved, was brought to nothing by a political accident
which compelled us prematurely to show our hand. Some

time previously, I had been adopted as Liberal candidate for Paisley without any anticipation that an early by-election would occur there. But now, in December, 1947, the death of Earl Baldwin and the consequent succession to the peerage of Oliver Baldwin, who then sat for Paisley as Labour member, caused a vacancy just too soon for us to publish our plans.

At the time, however, the by-election seemed to present me with an opportunity to anticipate events. It so happened that several leading members of the Paisley Unionist Association were also members of Scottish Convention and they immediately set about persuading their colleagues not to put up a Tory candidate in opposition to me. For a week or two letters appeared every day in the Paisley and Glasgow Press urging all who were opposed to the centralising policies of the Labour Government to unite behind my candidature, and, finally, the pressure was sufficient to bring about a joint meeting of the two Associations. I was invited to appear there and to state my views in the presence of both parties. It seemed wise that I should prepare my statement carefully and I therefore drew it up in numbered paragraphs in such a form that if it met with approval it could be adopted immediately as a joint declaration by the two parties. In large measure I used the paragraphs of the draft policy which had previously been prepared at our negotiating meetings and my statement included as paragraph 7 these words:—

"We believe that the distinctive national traditions and characteristics of Scotland are of great value to the United Kingdom and to the world, and that they constitute a priceless heritage of the Scottish people. If the process of centralising the economic control of Scotland in Whitehall is allowed to continue that heritage will be lost and our national existence endangered. We therefore consider that a measure of devolution in the government of Scotland is a matter of urgency.

"We recognise that there are differing opinions as to the extent to which such a measure is immediately practicable, but we urge that all parties in Scotland should seek to reach agreement on this question and that it should not be made an issue in party politics."

The joint meeting approved my statement enthusiastically and unanimously and, within a few minutes of my speaking, the typed copies which I had thoughtfully brought with me were signed by the office-bearers of both parties as a joint declaration and I was adopted by both as "National" candidate. No questions were asked as to what kind of "National" I was and when next day the news and the declaration were published it was only my old opponent the *Glasgow Herald* which chilled enthusiasm with doubt. Here is an extract from its leading article:

"The statement of policy approved by the two committees is, however, likely to arouse some misgivings. Paisley Unionists may question how far the declaration constitutes an agreed compromise, and how much of it consists simply of a restatement of Liberal policy on which the Unionist Association have been led to set their seal of approval. It also appears to assign an importance to the question of devolution in the government of Scotland disproportionate to that given to other and more pressing measures in the national interest; and the previous political affiliations of the joint candidate, Mr. MacCormick, have been such as to suggest that an early definition of his views on this matter is desirable."

Having thus weightily delivered itself of its warning the *Herald* could hardly with enthusiasm endorse my candidature and, thereafter, during the campaign it continued to display a caution which did everything but advise its Tory readers not to sup with the devil of Home Rule.

Although I believed with some reason that the steps I had been taking met with the approval both of Sir Archibald Sinclair and Lady Glen-Coats (who was, at the time, Chairman of the Scottish Liberal Party) and I had kept them informed as to what was happening, I was surprised when, immediately after the publication of the Paisley declaration, they denounced the pact with the Tories and advised Liberal voters in Paisley to have nothing to do with me. They thus destroyed all the hopes I had entertained of building up a permanent political alliance in Scotland which would have been powerful enough to secure a substantial degree of Home Rule. They are the last people in the world whom I could accuse of bad faith, yet I confess I was hurt by their denunciations. I believe they acted hastily under the impression that I had sold myself to the Tory Party and that, if I had had any opportunity to talk with them, I could have convinced them that my strategy was sound. They were influenced also by the negative attitude of the Liberal leaders in London and no doubt they may have felt, in any case, that my loyalties were far more bound up with Scottish self-government than with any political party. In this, of course, they were quite right, and as leaders of their Party they were perhaps justified in regarding me as unreliable. The truth is that I have never been able to understand such a thing as "party loyalty". Loyalty to friends, yes; loyalty to what one conceives to be right principle, yes; but loyalty to a party, which is a mere instrument to be used only for the attainment of an end, seems to me to be the negation of freedom. It is the subordination of a man's own judgement and conscience to the will of the majority. It can only lead to an unthinking acceptance of slogans instead of ideals and

to the prostitution of political endeavour to the satisfaction
of mere personal ambition.

In spite of my disappointment I entered with enthusiasm
into the fight in Paisley. My Labour opponent was Douglas
Johnstone, Q.C., then Solicitor-General for Scotland, and
I knew him well enough for us both to hit hard without
rancour. The campaign attracted attention from all quarters
and certainly no by-election in recent years was so much
publicised in the Press. It gave me some quiet pleasure to
find supporting me on my platform such well-known Tories
as Walter Elliot, Peter Thorneycroft, Manningham-Buller,
Lady Tweedsmuir (then Lady Grant) and many others who
had hitherto been distinguished as immoveable opponents of
Scottish Nationalism. I always took care to ensure that one
or other of my old comrades of Nationalist days would speak
at the same meeting just in case it might be necessary to
unsay one thing or re-emphasise another. Some of them, not
having studied or absorbed the "Paisley Declaration" simply
trotted out their good old well-tried Home Rule speeches but
the huge audiences which were now being attracted to the
meetings gave them far better cheer than was vouchsafed to
any other of my supporters. I remember with some amuse-
ment an occasion when the Town Hall was so packed that
at least 2,000 people could not find an entry and clamoured
outside in Gauze Street for an overflow meeting. The only way
to satisfy them was to send speakers one after another up to
a balcony far above the street. There was no loudspeaker
equipment and when it came my turn to go up I arrived in
time to see Walter Elliot give up the attempt to make himself
heard while his place was taken by my old friend John
McNicol who used to boast that he had the loudest voice in
the Scottish National Party. Sure enough, he had lost nothing
of his power and, in a full-throated roar, he drowned the
noise of traffic and delighted his huge audience with the old

wisecracks which I had heard in so many by-elections before. As he worked himself up to even mightier efforts he quite forgot both time and place and called upon the good people of Paisley, in such a voice as they had never heard before, to vote "for MacCormick and Scotland" and "down with London rule". I thought I saw a rather sickly smile on Walter Elliot's face as I stepped forward to relieve the strain on McNicol's throat!

Although Labour was by now very firmly entrenched in Paisley it looked for a while as though we might bring off a victory. But the very success of our campaign was perhaps our undoing. At the last moment, spurred by the obvious danger of defeat, the Labour Party exercised every ounce of its immense organisational strength and by pulling out to the polling booths every conceivable supporter they succeeded in defeating us by 25,000 votes to 21,000. Of course, I should have liked to win but, after all, it was a long way to travel from 1,600 votes in 1929 to 21,000 in 1948, and I was still standing, despite any change in labels, for precisely the same thing!

CHAPTER NINETEEN

DURING THE EARLY stages of the campaign in Paisley, the Committee of the Scottish National Assembly was not only putting the finishing touches to its proposals for Scottish self-government but was also preparing to meet Mr. Arthur Woodburn who was then Secretary of State for Scotland. We had requested a meeting with the Prime Minister but Mr. Attlee was involved in one of those periodic crises which marked the Labour Government's career. He begged to be excused, and passed us over to the Secretary of State. Arrangements were made for Mr. Woodburn to receive a deputation from the Committee on 9th January, 1948, in St. Andrew's House, which is the headquarters of Government in Edinburgh. As Chairman of the Committee it fell to me to lead the deputation and at first I felt some concern in case the Labour Party supporters among us would suddenly wash their hands of the whole business on account of my election activities. Any such course would have been quite illogical since we were all free to support or oppose any political party, but logic is seldom the mainspring of action, and there might well have been some feeling of resentment against me. Fortunately, however, the leading Labour man among us was the late William Gallacher (not the former Communist M.P. of the same name) who had been Chairman of the Scottish Co-operative Wholesale Society and who, in his retirement, was strongly backing the Home Rule movement. He was a man of wide sympathies and open mind and though he may not have liked what I was doing he recognised my right to do it and raised no partisan trouble in the Committee.

Indeed, as Vice-Chairman he was second in command of the deputation and when the meeting with Mr. Woodburn took place the case for our proposals was stated not only by myself but by Mr. Gallacher for Labour, the Duke of Montrose for the Liberals and Professor Dewar Gibb for the Conservatives. We thus preserved our united front and built up jointly a solid argument which was clearly not, in any way, a party attack upon the Labour Government.

Nevertheless, that is how Arthur Woodburn chose to regard our representations. I had never entertained much hope that he would do otherwise. He had for many years been the wholetime Secretary of the Scottish Labour Party Council and was a typical party bureaucrat, efficient, uninspired and totally incapable of looking at anything except through the narrow eyes of party bias. It was clear that he regarded the whole business as a Tory plot to embarrass the Socialist Government in general and himself in particular, and while he listened courteously enough to our arguments I could sense that he was very unlikely to be moved by them. Finally, he dismissed us with a few words which offered no encouragement. "The proposals," he said, "have obviously been carefully prepared and they are certainly the most complete and the most reasonable outline of a scheme for legislative devolution that I have seen. But I have yet to be convinced that there is any widespread demand in Scotland for such a measure. We have many more urgent things to tackle, such as the present food crisis, and I cannot promise that the Government will be able to give serious consideration to your demands. I have, however, made certain recommendations with regard to Scottish affairs which have met with the approval of my colleagues. I cannot disclose them now but they will be the subject of a White Paper which I shall present to Parliament within the next few weeks."

In due course his White Paper was published. It consisted

of three small pages and proposed nothing more than a slight extension of the Parliamentary time given to the Scottish estimates and modest improvement in the procedure of the Scottish Grand Committee. The Paisley campaign was still in progress and when I denounced Mr. Woodburn's policy as wholly inadequate for Scotland the *Glasgow Herald*, our leading Tory newspaper, solemnly quoted me in yet another leading article to prove that I should still be regarded as a Nationalist suspect by every good Unionist in Paisley. So much for the Tory plot against the Labour Party!

Now that it was clear beyond all doubt that the Government had no intention of fulfilling its pledges to Scotland we set about campaigning throughout the country with redoubled energy. In March, 1948, a second Assembly, even more representative than the first, gave almost unanimous approval to the proposals submitted by the Committee, and, by April, 1949, we felt that we had built up sufficient strength to justify our taking the next major step in the development of our policy. In that month a private and informal conference was held in what was then a small hotel in Aberfoyle. We brought into our councils there not only the leading members of the Assembly Committee but also a number of prominent Scottish Pressmen whom we knew were sympathetic to our cause. It was essential for what we had in mind that we should have as much help as possible from the Press and we wanted to have them in from the beginning.

After two days of discussion the decision was taken. We would launch for public signature a new Scottish Covenant and demonstrate beyond all doubt the truly widespread and deeply felt desire of the Scottish people for a Parliament of their own. We would try to do it in such way that a new enthusiasm would be generated among our people and a new conviction that, if they could only display their unity behind this one demand, the politicians in London could not continue to ignore them.

The Covenant was worded as follows:

"We, the people of Scotland who subscribe this Engagement, declare our belief that reform in the constitution of our country is necessary to secure good government in accordance with our Scottish traditions and to promote the spiritual and economic welfare of our nation.

"We affirm that the desire for such reform is both deep and widespread through the whole community, transcending all political differences and sectional interests, and we undertake to continue united in purpose for its achievement.

"With that end in view we solemnly enter into this Covenant whereby we pledge ourselves, in all loyalty to the Crown and within the framework of the United Kingdom, to do everything in our power to secure for Scotland a Parliament with adequate legislative authority in Scottish affairs."

It was thus both firm and moderate in its language and we believed was worded in such a way that no one, particularly in Scotland where things are usually carefully read before they are signed, would lightly put his name to it. It was designed not as a petition, but as a solemn undertaking by all who signed it that they would strive unceasingly for the attainment of our goal.

It was, of course, appropriate that the Covenant should be formally opened for signature at a third meeting of the National Assembly and we began to make arrangements accordingly. To give the occasion as much dignity as possible we booked the Church of Scotland Assembly Hall in Edinburgh, than which it seemed there could be no more fitting place to witness the launching of a new Covenant. For two centuries the Church had provided Scotland with the nearest approach she had to a Parliament and many matters of great moment to the people had been debated in that hall. Our invitations to the Assembly were sent to every public body in the country and the Press co-operated well in publicising the forthcoming event. Moreover, many prominent people in business, in the Church, in the trade unions and among the aristocracy who had never before committed themselves, now announced their intention to support the Covenant. In the result, when the Assembly opened on 29th October, 1949, nearly 1,200 delegates crowded into the debating chamber and the public galleries were filled by eager spectators.

The Scots are not naturally a demonstrative people, and it had not occurred to us to preconceive any form of ritual for the occasion. There were no banners on the walls, no shrieking slogans in the approaches, nor anything other than a somewhat untidy stall for the sale of literature at the entrance. The Teutons or the Slavs would have made the occasion one for the display of histrionic symbolism, but to the Celts, whose emotions are perhaps all the more powerful for their fear of displaying them, it was better to be douce and unpretentious, and slightly disorganised!

None the less, when the platform party, which had been hastily arranged a few minutes previously, filed in to sit below the throne of the King's High Commissioner, a sudden silence descended upon the hall. It was as though an awareness of solemnity and dedication had spontaneously entered the minds of all the people crowded there, and without any forethought I knew what ought to be done. Giving him only a brief whispered warning, I called upon Dr. Nevile Davidson, Minister of the Cathedral Church of Glasgow, to open our proceedings with prayer. He rose magnificently to the occasion, and in sonorous tones and unmatched eloquence he gave voice to the common purpose and united supplication of the people.

Thereafter, the Assembly addressed itself soberly but with deeply felt enthusiasm to its task. Delegate after delegate advanced to the rostrum to declare the reasons why he would sign the Covenant. Unknown district councillors rubbed shoulders and joined in pledges with men whose titles had sounded through all the history of Scotland. Working men from the docks of Glasgow or the pits of Fife spoke with the same voice as portly business-men in pin-striped trousers. It was such a demonstration of national unity as the Scots might never have hoped to see, and when, finally, the scroll upon which the Covenant was inscribed was unrolled for signature every person in the hall joined patiently in the queue to sign it. The first man to put his name to it was the Duke of Montrose whose ancestor, the Great Marquess, had been among the first to sign the old Covenant 300 years ago. It was with a thrill of pride that I, whose folk could trace their lineage to the time of the landing of Columcille on Iona, but whose forebears were simple crofters, followed immediately after him. Then one by one many of the true leaders of Scottish life and thought followed us, as well as hundreds of those more humble people who in Scotland, where we are all Jock Tamson's bairns, are the salt of the earth. I have no doubt that it was one of the great occasions in the long history of our nation, that whatever vicissitudes have befallen us and may yet befall, it marked a turning-point in the life of our people from which there will never be any going back.

That night I returned to my home in Glasgow exhausted but elated. I knew that the Covenant campaign, for which we had so long prepared, would be successful beyond my most sanguine hopes. Indeed, from the point of view of practical arrangement, I suspected that we had failed to measure adequately the popular response to our appeal for signatures and though it was long after business hours I telephoned to our printer at his home and asked him to set in hand immediately on Monday morning the printing of 10,000 additional signature sheets. Even then I little suspected that this would be the first of many a hurried order for more copies.

In the first wave of popular enthusiasm no less than 50,000 signatures to the Covenant were collected within a week of the Assembly meeting. Collected is really the wrong word for we were, by no means, properly organised to canvass for signatures on so vast a scale. We were, in fact, overwhelmed both in our Glasgow and Edinburgh offices by the constant surge of people claiming both to add their own names and to take forms for the signature of their friends and neighbours. The 10,000 copies which I had ordered, each with lines for eighteen signatures, were distributed as fast as they came off the printing press, not by post or at random but solely to people who demanded them. When I now look back and remember how often we were accused by the leading opponents of our movement of having trailed the Covenant in the streets for irresponsible signatures, I am amused to think that our main concern in those first few days was to put a brake on the spontaneous rush of unknown supporters till we should have sufficient forms to satisfy them.

This first enthusiasm, of course, might soon have spent itself but suddenly we received help from a most unsuspected source. One night, about ten days after the Covenant had been launched, I was awakened by the clamant ringing of my telephone bell. The caller was the chief reporter of one of the Glasgow daily newspapers.

"We're just hearing from London," he said, "that you are, at this moment, being accused in the House of Commons of inciting the people of Scotland to violence. We'd like your comments."

"What's been happening?" I asked rather sleepily.

"Arthur Woodburn has just been saying in the House that you're really a wolf in sheep's clothing. That you've managed to rope in a lot of respectable people to the Covenant movement under false pretences. That you're really a violent person who wouldn't hesitate to blow up Downing Street and the Palace of Westminster itself."

I admit that I was taken aback! Although perforce I had taken a considerable part in the Scottish movement, I had never relished personal publicity and was by nature far too timid to like the thought of meeting such an accusation by a Minister of Cabinet rank.

"How does he make that out?" I asked, as calmly as I could.

"He's been quoting from your speeches," came the answer. "Apparently you once said that a bomb in Downing Street would do more good than all the sweet reasonableness in the world."

Vague memories of phrases I might have used long ago to point my arguments began to surge in my mind. But at the same time the schoolboy sense of guilt, which had been the seed of fear, left me entirely. I knew at once that the man who was accusing me, protected though he was by all the privilege of Parliament, was blundering to his own destruction. I knew with complete certainty that nothing I had ever said in all my life could be construed as a call to indiscriminate violence. There is no idea, no thought of any human advancement, for which I would shed one drop of innocent human blood. I have never been able to think of men as mere symbols created in the image of their own ideologies. Therefore, I knew that, even in the indiscretions of hundreds of speeches, I could not have been guilty. And with the same

certainty I knew that Arthur Woodburn, by making such
wild accusations in Parliament, had ensured the continued
success of the Covenant campaign.

It afterwards transpired that the two speeches from which
Woodburn had quoted could not, by any flight of imagination, bear the interpretation he had put upon them. In one,
delivered some years previously in Edinburgh, I had said
that though the Scots might more quickly reach their goal
if some young enthusiast would explode a bomb outside
10 Downing Street, they preferred the slower but more
rational methods of considered argument. In the other,
which was made in the course of the Paisley by-election, I
had assured the *Glasgow Herald* that, if I were elected, I
would carry no "Scottish Nationalist bombs" into the
House of Commons!

The whole upshot of Woodburn's gunpowder plot was
that the Covenant suddenly became the most urgent topic
of conversation in Scotland. His speech in Parliament was
headlined in every Scottish newspaper and my reply, which
consisted only in quoting accurately in their context the
statements from which he had deduced my violent disposi-
tion, made him a laughing-stock throughout the length and
breadth of the land. Indeed, within a very short time he
became so much of an embarrassment to the Labour
Government that he was removed from office and replaced
by Hector McNeil. It was significant that Hector, an old
schoolfellow and college mate of my own, had won his spurs
in his dealings with Vyshinsky at the United Nations, before
he was appointed to pacify his fellow countrymen. But by the
time of his appointment the number of signatures to the
Covenant was rising towards 2,000,000 and the task of
damping down the fire of Scotland's rediscovered nationhood
was beyond even his smooth diplomacy to accomplish.

CHAPTER TWENTY

THE EVENTS WHICH I am now describing are so recent that I find it difficult to write about them in a proper sequence, whether of logic or of time. So many things happened in the two years of Covenant campaigning, so many unexpected people joined us, became prominent among us and faded away again after the first enthusiasm had waned, that I feel as though I were looking back on a film which has been speeded up to supernatural tempo. My own life at that time seems to have been made up entirely of interminable journeys from one end of Scotland to the other, from Scotland to London and even across the Atlantic and over half the American continent. In two years I spoke at more than 600 meetings and wherever I went there were eager crowds and queues to sign the Covenant.

The biggest political meeting I have ever seen in my life was held in the St. Andrews Halls in Glasgow three weeks after the Covenant had been launched. The main hall which officially sits 3,000 people was packed far beyond capacity; the lesser hall, hastily booked for an overflow, was crowded too; and literally thousands of people milled around outside demanding an opportunity to sign the Covenant. Although it was a bitterly cold night tables were put outside on the pavement, and, for two hours, a continuous stream of douce Glasgow citizens filed past to proclaim by their signatures their faith in their Scottish nationhood. There has never been so spontaneous a demonstration by Scots people on any matter of public interest as there was that night, and Glasgow did no more than lead the way for every town and village in the land. Those who now pooh-pooh the Covenant should remember that, though it takes the Scots a long time to make up their minds about anything, they do not easily change again. The resolution which was then displayed is now as firm as ever and waits only an opportunity for its more emphatic expression.

In less than six months we were able to announce that 1,000,000 people had signed the Covenant, and thus armed we convened another National Assembly. It met in April 1950, in an atmosphere of intense and expectant enthusiasm. With complete unanimity it adopted two principal resolutions, the first that commissioners should be appointed to interview both the Prime Minister and the Leader of the Opposition and the second that, if no satisfactory assurances were given by the Parliamentary leaders a petition should be presented directly to the King.

In the result, neither Mr. Attlee nor Mr. Churchill agreed to meet the Assembly's commissioners and both of them referred us to their deputies—in Mr. Attlee's case, Hector McNeil, who was by this time Secretary of State for Scotland, and, in Mr. Churchill's case, Mr. James Stuart, who now (1954) occupies that office, and Mr. Walter Elliot.

On the advice of my own committee I declined to meet these substitutes but delegated others to do so. We naturally expected no satisfaction from such interviews but the force of public opinion was so strong that we could not be entirely ignored. Hector McNeil immediately intimated the appointment of a Committee of Enquiry to examine the financial relationship between England and Scotland, and the Scottish Unionist Party went one better by producing a pamphlet on *Scottish Control of Scottish Affairs* which, among other promises included a pledge to appoint a Royal Commission to examine all the functions of Government in Scotland.

It is only by such small yet significant stages that the

parties entrenched in power can be moved by public opinion. The important thing, however, and the thing which justifies even an imperfect democracy, is that they can be moved at all! Having been in minority movements of one kind or another all my life I am in a position to speak with some authority in this matter. I would say of Britain, and I admit that, in this respect, I am stretching the meaning of that proud name, that I would rather be in a minority in this island than anywhere else in the world. We grumble and complain against the powers that be; we prove to our own complete satisfaction that we are unfairly stifled and repressed; but we go on talking, and by infinitesimal stages our talk pushes our unwilling rulers along the road we want to go. I think it is the genius of the English that they are capable of being pushed; I think it is the genius of the Celtic peoples that we keep on pushing with all the fervour of minorities; and I think that these islands have given more to the world than any other conglomeration simply because we have here learned the meaning of give and take. I want a Scottish Parliament and a resurgence of Scottish nationality not because I hate the English (though sometimes, of course, I do) but because I believe that the new and spurious and artificial nationalism of Greater London requires a counterpoise if what we all unconsciously recognise as British is to survive. The British Isles are, when all is said and done, the last refuge of those Europeans who refused to be conquered and, therefore, made their getaway! English and Scots, Welsh and Irish, whatever we are and whatever our origins, we have learned subconsciously to depend upon each other and to need even our rivalries with each other to make life interesting and worth while. We have become a microcosm of the world in which even hatred and intolerance have among us always been tempered by a sense of guilt. We can hang, disembowel and quarter the so-called traitor in our midst, and we can then put up a statue to commemorate his heroism!

Following the meagre results of our meetings with the two parties our next step was to invite them to agree to take a national plebiscite in Scotland. A questionnaire to this effect was addressed to the Prime Minister, the Leader of the Opposition and to all Scottish members of Parliament. The official replies which we received are worth quoting.

The Government replied through Mr. Hector McNeil on 27th July, 1950, as follows:

"The questionnaire has been, I am sure, read with interest by all of us but in the view of my colleagues and myself the issues involved are complicated and cannot be dealt with by simple question and answer of the kind contained in the questionnaire, or by a plebiscite. I should add too that it is our view that constitutional change in this country is considered and settled by the normal process of Parliamentary democracy."

I replied to Mr. McNeil as follows:

"MY DEAR HECTOR,—Your letter of 27th July, addressed to Councillor Robert Gray, was read at a meeting of the National Covenant Committee on Saturday last. I was requested to reply to you saying that the committee find it difficult to understand why, at the very least, the first question on their questionnaire cannot be dealt with by the Prime Minister and yourself.

"That question, you will remember, simply asked whether, if the Scottish people clearly showed their desire for a Scottish Parliament they were, in your view, entitled to have their desire realised. Are we to take it from your reply that such a question does not permit of a simple answer? Does it follow that there is some doubt in your or the Prime Minister's mind as to whether the people of Scotland are the best judges on the matter of Scottish self-government?

"You will readily appreciate the importance of this question if you will relate it to the last paragraph of your letter. You there state your view that 'constitutional change in this country is considered and settled by the normal processes of Parliamentary democracy'.

"There are in Parliament 554 English and Welsh members as against 71 Scottish Members. It follows that in the 'normal processes of Parliamentary democracy' a situation might readily arise in which, although a majority of Scottish members representing a majority of their country-men supported a measure to achieve self-government, they would be helpless in the face of an adverse English majority. This is no mere hypothetical case, since similar situations have already arisen in the past.

"My Committee therefore suggest that in this matter something more than 'the normal processes of Parliamentary democracy' must be taken into account, namely the desire of the Scottish people, if such be proved, to govern themselves.

"It is thus of the utmost importance that the Government's attitude to our question should be clearly defined. If no answer is given it must be supposed that in the case of Scotland, unlike that of any other nation, the wishes of her people are, in the Government's view, irrelevant.

"I propose to send this letter to the Press, and also to distribute copies of our first question to all English and Welsh members of Parliament in the hope that their answers will show their willingness to recognise that revision of the nature of the Union between England and Scotland, if desired by one of the partners in the Union, must be dealt with on principles which transcend any narrow interpretation of the 'normal processes of Parliamentary democracy."

A few days after this correspondence had been published Mr. Churchill as Leader of the Opposition and Mr. James Stuart as Chairman of the Scottish Unionist Members of Parliament also replied to us. Their letters, too, are sufficiently important to be worthy of quotation. Mr. Churchill said:

"I have received your letter of 8th July, for which I thank you.

"In reply, I would inform you that I have seen and approved the letter sent to you by the chairman of the Scottish Unionist Members' Committee on behalf of Scottish Unionist and Liberal Unionist members of Parliament. This letter expresses my own view, and there is nothing I can add to it."

Mr. Stuart's letter, which had thus received Mr. Churchill's *imprimatur* was in the following terms:

"On behalf of the Scottish Unionist Members' Committee I write in reply to the letter, dated 12th July, 1950, which you addressed individually to Scottish Unionist and Liberal Unionist Members of Parliament, and to the questionnaire which you enclosed therewith.

"Having carefully considered these documents, we wish to make our position clear to all.

"If the people of Scotland were ultimately to decide in favour of a Scottish Parliament no one could gainsay them.

"We do not, however, hold the view that such extremely complex matters can properly be determined either by plebiscite or by reference to the number of signatures affixed to any document. The constitutional methods by which the people in our democracy can make their wishes known and effective are well understood, generally respected, in constant use, and available to all shades of opinion.

"We stand by the carefully considered official statement of policy issued last year. We believe this policy to be in the best interests of our own country, of Great Britain, and of the Commonwealth and Empire."

The matters of discussion then begun are only now, at the time of writing, beginning to crystallise the whole subject of argument between the Covenant movement and the political parties and I therefore think it worth while to quote my replies. To Mr. Churchill I wrote on 7th August, 1950, in these terms:

"It will be most satisfactory to my committee to learn that the greatest living Englishman has associated himself with the statement that 'if the people of Scotland were ultimately to decide in favour of a Scottish Parliament no one could gainsay them'. But, with your unrivalled experience of Parliamentary and political affairs, I think you will agree that a method should be devised to enable the Scottish people to record such a decision beyond the possibility of any doubt. It has seemed to my committee, that a plebiscite would be the best and fairest method, and it surely rests with those who are opposed to a plebiscite to suggest an alternative.

"I shall, therefore, be much obliged if you will consider the terms of my letter to Mr. Stuart.

"May I add that my 'Committee are still most hopeful that you will yet be able to meet their representatives so that they may put before you the reasons why this whole matter should be dealt with above the level of ordinary party politics."

My letter to Mr. Stuart was as follows:

"DEAR SIR,—Your letter of 2nd instant, addressed to our Vice-Chairman, has been passed to me, and I shall present it to my Committee as soon as possible. In the meantime, however, I am not quite clear as to your meaning, and it will be helpful if you will clarify your terms.

"You say that if the people of Scotland were ultimately to decide in favour of a Scottish Parliament, no one could gainsay them. I do not understand what you mean by the word 'ultimately'. A sufficiently large number of Scottish electors have now signed the Scottish Covenant, to make it appear probable that the people of Scotland have already decided in favour of a Scottish Parliament. Lest there be any doubt of that, my Committee have proposed that a plebiscite be taken or that some alternative means of testing opinion should be suggested by those who are opposed to a plebiscite.

"You have made no such alternative suggestion. You have merely stated that 'the constitutional methods by which the people in our democracy can make their wishes known and effective are well understood', but although I have made a close study of this matter over many years I confess that I do not understand how these methods operate on a question of this nature.

"Do you mean that when a majority of Scottish constituencies return members to Parliament who are pledged to support a measure of Scottish self-government this will be accepted as evidence that the people have decided in favour of a Scottish Parliament?

"I should be very glad to be assured that this is your meaning. I am, however, bound to point out that on more than one occasion in the past such majorities have been elected, but their mandate has not been accepted by the House of Commons.

"Your objection to a plebiscite appears to be that 'such an extremely complex matter' cannot suitably be dealt with in this manner. If you are suggesting that a complex matter can more easily be understood by the electors during a General Election campaign in which many other complex issues are also involved, than when it is referred to their vote in a dispassionate way and without the stress of party feeling, then I find it very difficult to follow your reasoning.

"On the other hand, it may be your view that the question as to whether the Scottish people want a Parliament of their own can better be decided for them by some committee of experts than by themselves.

"If this is indeed your view, and the view of your colleagues, I invite you to say so clearly, as the Scottish people have a right to know what their elected representatives think of them.

"The method of testing opinion by plebiscite on a matter of general principle, such as Scottish self-government, which transcends party differences is, furthermore, not foreign to our constitutional practice.

"At a time recently when Newfoundland was under the authority of the United Kingdom Government, the future status of that province was determined by plebiscite authorised by legislation passed in the United Kingdom Parliament. The local veto arrangements made under the Temperance (Scotland) Act, 1913, also constitute a form of plebiscite designed to deal with a matter which stood outside of ordinary party conflict.

"In the light of these considerations I ask you and your colleagues to reconsider our questionnaire and, if possible, to let me have your further observations before 26th August, when my Committee again meets.

"I propose to send a copy of this letter to Mr. Churchill and also to send the correspondence to the Press."

I leave it to my readers to decide where in the course of these exchanges between the Covenant movement and the English parties the strength of logic lay. They were important to us at the time for they called forth strong leading articles in favour of our point of view from such respectable and cautious newspapers as the *Scotsman* and the *Economist*. These articles are a fair reflection of the atmosphere of opinion which the success of the Covenant had by now created and I have therefore included them among the appendices to this volume.

In the meantime, despite all the evidences of the continuing growth of our movement, there were already developing signs of disaffection among our own ranks. At least one very prominent supporter withdrew his signature from the Covenant in circumstances and for reasons which showed how little he understood the necessities of political action or the value of harnessing opinion far beyond the shores of Scotland.

CHAPTER TWENTY-ONE

THE CONTROVERSIES which I have just recorded did not proceed without the interruptions which were the necessary concomitant of what had become a world-wide campaign. No sooner had the Covenant attracted its first 1,000,000 signatures than the Press of every nation began to take an interest in our Scottish affairs. Their representatives came to us from every quarter of the globe—from Europe, from Asia and Australasia and from both of the Americas. They came seeking information, and, as often as not, they failed to digest what they found and spilled it out in very frothy ink. In a French newspaper, for example, I was described as having eyes which could only be compared with Mussolini's and hands the same as Hitler's! In the West German equivalent of *Picture Post* I was portrayed as a sullen backroom boy with a genius for organisation. In a newspaper in Vancouver, with even more inaccuracy, I was accused of being an Irish barrister, born in Dublin, who had come over to Scotland to stir up more trouble for the English.

These extraordinary pictures of myself were, of course, only to be expected from journalists whose trade it was to portray deep-seated movements of opinion in irrelevant personal terms. Though I disliked them I did not give any weight to them and was well enough pleased that after 200 years of anonymity Scotland was again coming into the news.

Matters took on a different colour, however, when we were informed by a friendly American journalist, that the British Consul in an important U.S. city, had so far committed himself as to inform an enquirer in writing, on official British Government stationery, that the Covenant movement was wholly irresponsible and unrepresentative of Scottish opinion. We thought that the Consul had far exceeded his duties and had ventured into fields of judgement which were clearly beyond his proper sphere, and, accordingly, we protested in the strongest possible terms to the Foreign Office. I believe that the Consul in question was privately reprimanded for allowing such a letter as he had written ever to reach our hands, but, so far as we were concerned, we were given no public satisfaction.

The incident served to convince several members of the Covenant Committee that a delegation should be sent to the United States and Canada to explain in unmistakable terms precisely what we aimed to achieve. We felt that misunderstanding across the Atlantic would have its repercussions back at home, and many of us believed also that a little pressure from the New World would do no harm to our cause. I cannot say that I was personally very enthusiastic about the idea, but matters came to a head when three members of our Committee, Mr. William Graham, Mr. Robert Turpie and Mr. John J. Campbell volunteered to make the trip at their own expense. All three of them were, like myself, practising solicitors in Glasgow and, unfortunately, they were all very recent recruits to our cause who had joined us in the first flush of the Covenant's success. While I had no doubts about their *bona fides* and their enthusiastic energy had done much to help the movement, they were inexperienced in our propaganda and unaccustomed to speaking either on the public platform or to the Press on the aims of Scottish Convention. I felt that since they were obviously eager, and, indeed, determined to go it would be as well that someone else should accompany them and, *faute de mieux*, I agreed to go with them myself. A few misgivings about the wisdom of our journey were expressed by some Committee members but, on the whole, our offer to undertake so heavy a task and to finance it out of our own pockets was welcomed by our colleagues. Accordingly, after making a few preliminary contacts in the U.S.A. and Canada by post, we duly embarked upon the *Queen Mary* at Southampton on 24th June, 1950.

We had no sooner boarded the liner and gone through the preliminaries of checking our luggage into our cabins, than I was surprised to discover that we had a distinguished fellow-passenger. As I walked in exploratory fashion along the promenade deck my eye was caught by a small and heavily muffled figure sitting in a hunched attitude on a deck-chair. Something vaguely familiar about the shape of his head made me look at him twice, and, although his face was almost completely covered, I was certain that it was my old acquaintance Lord Beaverbrook whom I had not seen since the very early days of the National Party.

Although I felt sure that I could not be mistaken I hesitated to approach him. He looked like someone who was trying to travel incognito, and, in any case, he might have forgotten all about me. I thought, therefore, that I would first make doubly certain of his identity and then hope for an opportunity to talk to him during the voyage. I wanted to talk to him for two good reasons. The first was that, in my former encounters with him, I had developed a real affection for him and the second was that the *Scottish Daily Express* had been little more than lukewarm in its attitude to the Covenant. By now it had a very large daily circulation in Scotland and if I could win again the interest of its proprietor I might with one lucky blow justify our whole excursion.

I confided my discovery to Willie Graham, and told him that I was not quite certain in the matter of identity. Graham is a real "go-getter" who has a natural instinct for pulling ropes, and I knew that he would soon find the means of resolving whatever shred of doubt I had. At first he met

with stout denials in the Purser's office that any such person
as Lord Beaverbrook was on board, but, with a little judicious
tipping, he soon learned that I was right, although neither
His Lordship's name nor the names of any of his party were
on the printed passenger list. Apparently he was tired and ill
and wanted to be left severely alone during the voyage which
was the first stage of a journey to Jamaica for rest and
recuperation.

In these circumstances I felt very hesitant, in spite of the
persuasions of my colleagues, to make a frontal attack on his
privacy. I could only hope that in the course of perambula-
tions round the decks we might on some occasion meet face
to face, and, if he recognised and remembered me, he might,
of his own accord, desire to speak to me. Unfortunately, he
seemed to keep pretty closely to his own suite and for a couple
of days I saw nothing of him. My friends were becoming
quite restive and highly critical of what they called my
timidity but what seemed to me to be no more than good
manners. I still protested that if Beaverbrook knew I was on
the ship and wished to talk to me he would send for me. To
which they replied reasonably enough that if I did not
approach him he could never know that I was there.

On the third afternoon I was passing the time in the ship's
cinema when the programme was suddenly interrupted by
the booming voice of a loudspeaker calling upon Mr.
So-and-So to go at once to the cable office to receive an
urgent message. Such a summons would, of course, be heard
in every part of the ship and even in the staterooms, and
immediately it occurred to me that here was a method by
which I could make known the presence of the Covenant
delegation.

Without waiting to see the end of the film I proceeded at
once to the cable office and sent a cryptic message to Robert
Gray in Glasgow asking him immediately to cable to me on

the *Queen Mary*. Both economy and tact prevented me making any other explanation than that I wanted to be cabled and that it must be addressed to me as a member of the Scottish Covenant delegation. I knew he would be puzzled but I knew he would respond with something suitable for the occasion and I reckoned that before long the fact that I was on board the *Queen Mary* as a member of the Scottish Covenant delegation would be proclaimed from every loudspeaker on the ship, and could not fail to reach the ears of my quarry!

Alas, the best laid schemes are always the ones to go wrong. Late that evening I was passing through the main hall to have a final saunter round the promenade deck, when a bright-eyed page-boy emerged from the cable office, and, after a couple of glances at me, saluted and enquired in good Glasgow speech if I was Mr. MacCormick. When I admitted my identity he handed me my cable! With a heavy heart at the thought of the money I had wasted I praised the lad for his efficiency and added a handsome tip to what had already been thrown away!

Thereafter, I had no alternative but to yield to the pressure of my companions. I wrote a brief letter to Lord Beaverbrook explaining that a Covenant delegation was travelling to America and that, having seen him on board, I thought he might be interested to hear about the progress of our movement at first hand. I left it to himself to decide whether he would see me or not.

Within half an hour of his receiving this note, which I bribed my bedroom steward to have delivered, I found myself speaking on the telephone to one of his secretaries.

"Lord Beaverbrook is very pleased to know you are on board," she said. "Would you care to see him in the garden lounge this evening while dinner is in progress—His Lordship usually takes his evening walk then while the decks are quiet."

That is how I came to meet Beaverbrook again for the first time since that memorable occasion twenty years ago when he had given me and my cause his blessing. He was accompanied in the garden lounge by a charming young woman who, I soon learned, was his granddaughter, Lady Jean Campbell, daughter of the present Duke of Argyll. I need not have worried about his not remembering me. He soon showed that he was completely up-to-date about all that was happening in Scotland, and, as usual, he fired a series of searching questions at me about the Covenant and my quarrel in 1942 with the National Party. He reminded me that the *Express* had backed me strongly in the Paisley election and asked if I was satisfied with its present attitude to our campaign. I was bold enough to say that, too frequently, its Scottish leading articles damned us with faint praise and that it gave less news space than certain others to reports of our activities. I knew and was friendly with his Scottish Editor, Sandy Trotter, and had no criticism to make of him, but I assumed that, considering the limits imposed on him by shortage of space he was simply accepting a general line of policy laid down in London.

Whereupon His Lordship assured me with something very like a youthful twinkle in his eye, that he was now an old frail man and had very little to do with the daily running of his newspaper. If I had any complaint to make he would be delighted to see if he could do anything about it. We had a pleasant, completely inconclusive conversation for about an hour, but when early diners began to appear again on the promenade deck he rose to go back to the privacy of his own quarters. I strolled along the deck with him.

"I'm too old to be of any use to you," he said, before we parted. "It's people like my granddaughter here that you want to enlist. She's keen about her Scottish ancestry and I'm sure she'll be all for Home Rule. Send some of your literature down to her tonight and she'll tell me all about it in the morning."

I learned from Sandy Trotter on my return to Glasgow two weeks later that the "old man" had spoken to him as soon as he reached New York. He had told him to be sure to give us a fair show in the *Express* and then had chuckled. "Tell MacCormick he should be a better Scotsman. When I offered him a drink he asked for pale sherry! That's no advertisement for Scotch!"

CHAPTER TWENTY-TWO

I DO NOT LOOK back to those nine days on the North American continent with any great pride or pleasure. We visited and spoke to Scottish societies in New York, Washington, Chicago and Toronto and were successful even in setting up Covenant committees both in the U.S.A. and Canada, but I had a strong feeling that these committees would be ephemeral and their efforts to acquaint the American people with the problems of Scotland abortive.

The Scot in America is a somewhat peculiar creature. He loves to display, and even to exaggerate his Scottish accent, he joins clan societies and St. Andrew's clubs, and in his collective capacity he often, as in Chicago, makes magnificent provision for those of his countrymen who have fallen upon evil times in the land of their adoption. He is shrewdly aware of the advantages of being a Scot in a community which has always admired and respected the Scottish character and he is quite prepared to exploit the popularity of his motherland for his own advancement. But, although he remains fervently attached to Scotland the ties which bind him are those merely of kailyard sentimentality and it would never occur to him that he has any serious responsibility towards the home which nurtured him, gave him his education and provided him with a unique chance in the world. He is forever pointing out that his societies in America are merely charitable organisations and that they never, upon any account, dabble in politics. He is, therefore, not the kind of person who can easily be persuaded to take more than a fleeting interest in the active upsurge of national feeling which is now changing the face of Scotland. As often as not he emigrated in a mood of hopeless despair for the future of his country and he still in his heart of hearts regards it as a good place from which to have escaped.

Of course, we were well and hospitably received wherever we went and our audiences were obviously well-pleased to hear something about the Covenant which, if they had known anything at all about it, they had largely misunderstood. They were willing to display a polite sympathy but it seemed to me highly unlikely that they would ever do anything very serious to help us. In the event, my fears were justified and I cannot claim that we made any very deep mark on the life of the American-Scottish community.

In Washington we met a number of Senators and Congressmen and were even entertained to lunch in the Capitol. Our talks there did, I believe, serve a useful purpose in helping some of the leading men in American public life to understand our aims. Most of them had heard or read vaguely about the Covenant but they pictured it as a wild movement out to wreck the British Empire and to cut all ties with England. When we pointed out that we aimed at little more self-government than was possessed by every state in the Union they were quick to express their sympathy with us and to squeeze whatever drops of Scottish blood were in their veins to the surface.

When we crossed the border into Canada we found a much warmer welcome than in the States. Robert Turpie had gone there ahead of the rest of us and in Ottawa he had met several members of the Dominion Government, all of whom had expressed the keenest interest in the progress of the Home Rule cause. When we all arrived in Toronto we were received by the Mayor and Town Council in the City Chambers and I was asked to speak to them on the Covenant for half an hour. The Mayor was himself a Scot from Dundee and it seemed that most of his colleagues were either Scottish-born or of Scottish descent. Our visit to the town fortunately coincided with the Annual Convention there of all the Scottish clan societies in North America and again I was given the opportunity to speak, on this occasion, to several hundred delegates who came from almost every important town in the States and Canada.

We had no difficulty in forming a strong Covenant Committee in Toronto and I am sure that, if we had been able to stay in Canada for two weeks instead of two nights, we should have won important support for our cause. It was quite obvious that, so far as Canada is not French, it is very largely Scottish and extremely proud of the fact. On a vast and continental scale its physical relationship with its neighbour to the south is not unlike that of Scotland with England and it is very easy for any Canadian to understand the desire of the Scots not to lose their identity by submergence in any greater whole.

Canada is, without doubt, one of the great and truly liberal nations of the future and although we in Scotland can no longer afford the huge tide of westward emigration which still leaves our shores every year, we have good reason to be proud of the contribution which our kinsmen have made to Canada's fulfilment.

But the highlight of the tour, so far as I was concerned, was not in Canada—it was across the Great Lakes in Chicago. One of our principal objects was to try to interest the American Press in Scottish affairs and while we were in Washington I recalled that the *Chicago Tribune* correspondent at home had often sought long interviews from me and had told me that his proprietor, Colonel Robert McCormick, had specially asked for these despatches. It now occurred to me, since we were going to Chicago and had no prior contacts there, that I might telephone to the Colonel and ask him, if he showed any interest, to lay on a Press conference for us on our arrival.

From Washington, therefore, I put through a long-distance call to the *Tribune* office and asked to speak to Colonel McCormick. At first I was told that this was impossible but when I was asked for my name and said it was MacCormick there was an immediate change at the other end of the line. Colonel McCormick was not in the office but if I would hold on they would find him for me wherever he was. After a short wait, during which I could hear the telephonist trying various numbers, I found myself speaking to the Colonel himself. I told him my name and business and said I would be arriving with a companion in Chicago at eight o'clock next Sunday morning.

"I'll be pleased to see you," he said. "Come right up to my town house for breakfast and I'll have porridge on the table for you. After that I'll see that you meet the best Pressmen in Chicago."

In due course, accompanied by Willie Graham, I presented myself early on Sunday morning at the Colonel's home in the millionaire quarter of Chicago.

We were received hospitably, indeed even enthusiastically, by Mrs. McCormick who explained that her husband was not an early riser.

"But I'm so delighted to meet anyone from Scotland!" she exclaimed. "My ancestors were Mathesons from Inverness-shire but Bertie's not sure whether he's 'Scotch' or Irish. He's so jealous of me because I've got a tartan and he can't find one for the McCormick's."

I had taken the precaution to look the Colonel up in the American *Who's Who*, and, having learned from his entry that he was a Presbyterian, I thought it a safe bet that his family was of Scottish origin.

"The trouble about the MacCormick's," I said, "is that our family is so ancient that it pre-dates the development of the clan system in Scotland.[1] But your husband has every right to wear a tartan if he chooses. The MacCormick's, although they are not a sept of the clan, have the privilege of wearing the tartan of the MacLaines of Lochbuie."

"Won't Bertie just be delighted to hear that!" she exclaimed. "He's been dying to know about the history of his name. You're the very man he would like to meet."

When finally the Colonel came down to breakfast I was immediately persuaded to repeat what I had said, and to tell him more. Whatever his reputation is as a fire-eating Anglophobe and American nationalist he is a most delightful person to meet. He is tall and soldierly, he speaks without a trace of Transatlantic accent, and his manner of grave courtesy is in the best tradition of the Virginian aristocracy to which he belongs. When I had told him about his tartan he asked eagerly for more information and so I told him the whole story.

Long ago, in the fifteenth century there were two closely related clans who held sway in the islands of Mull and Iona— the McLeans of Duart and the MacLaines of Lochbuie.

During the infancy of one of the chiefs of Lochbuie, who became known to Highland history as Murachadh Gearr, or Murdoch the Short, his wicked uncle the Chief of Duart usurped his possessions and Murdoch was smuggled to Ireland by his foster-mother to save his life. After the usual fashion of such tales, the hero grew up to be superlatively strong, brave and athletic and he resolved to return with only a few companions to his native Isle of Mull to recover his lost possessions. After many adventures, which to this day are the subject of long tales at *ceilidhs* round the peat-fire hearths of Mull, Murdoch succeeded in regaining his ancestral Castle of Moy by the shores of Lochbuie. His constant

[1]This, incidentally, is quite true. The surname is undoubtedly very old, and, in the *Book of Deer* there is a record of one Gillechrist MacCormick having witnessed a Charter in the year 1124.

companion-in-arms throughout all his struggles was one MacCormick, very likely his foster-brother, and out of gratitude for his help Murdoch had carved upon the stone above the lintel these words: "*Biadh is deoch do MhacCormaig*" which signify in English, "Meat and drink to the MacCormick".

That was the story which I told over the breakfast table in Chicago, and I could not help thinking that it was very strange to be telling it in these sumptuous surroundings and to so eager an audience when I myself had heard it so often in my childhood sitting in the murk of the peat smoke in some black house in Mull.

There was no doubt about the eagerness of my audience. I went into greater detail in the telling than I have done here and both the Colonel and his wife were quite spellbound, while Willie Graham was looking at me with astonishment, having never dreamt that a sedate Glasgow lawyer could so appropriately dig up the obscure history of a barren corner of the Western Isles.

When I ended the story with the quotation from Moy Castle Colonel McCormick almost leapt to his feet.

"I've been wondering for years where that motto came from," he exclaimed. "Do you know that I have it carved in stone above the cocktail bar in my country house! You positively must come out and see it and tell me whether the Gaelic is properly rendered."

I murmured that I had planned to meet the Press in Chicago but he waved all objections aside.

"I'll have the Press here inside half an hour," he said. "You can talk to them for as long as you like but you must spend the rest of the day with me."

He was as good as his word. We had hardly finished breakfast before a bevy of top-ranking reporters and Press photographers had arrived, and, after half an hour of close cross-examination from them, we were ready for the road.

I am always interested in the idiosyncrasies of men of such highly marked individuality as Colonel McCormick, and, as we sped in a huge car along the thirty miles of broad highway which leads to the village of Whitton, it amused me to note that each seat in the car was provided with straps as in an aeroplane and in front of each was a receptacle filled with writing-pads and rows of neatly sharpened pencils. Apparently the Colonel was accustomed to fast travel but was not above taking precautions both for comfort and safety.

His home at Whitton was a very beautiful colonial style mansion set in magnificent grounds, complete with swimming pool, fully equipped cinema and all mod. cons. Never in my life had I been in any place which so quietly and so tastefully but so manifestly oozed wealth and I cannot say that I found it unpleasant.

Sure enough, in stonework set above a magnificent cocktail bar, carved in elaborate Celtic lettering, appeared the legend *"Biadh is deoch do MhacCormaig"*.

When I had duly admired it and confirmed the Gaelic spelling Mrs. McCormick said:

"Now for the drink. We'll have the food afterwards! I think a 'Scotch Mist' would be the right thing for the occasion."

I had never heard of a "Scotch Mist" except as a peculiarly unpleasant form of rain but it turned out to be a good stiff whisky with finely crushed ice stirred up in it, and very acceptable on a hot day in June.

In these exotic surroundings, and standing beneath the slogan which had first been carved so far away and so long ago we solemnly toasted the MacCormicks, the Clan MacLaine and the memory of Murachadh Gearr!

For the rest of the day we idled in luxuriant ease and in the evening we dined on the veranda in company with the local Presbyterian Minister whom the Colonel had called up because his name was Stewart and he too was Scots. It was a delightful meal served on pure gold plate. Mrs. McCormick whispered to me that we were highly honoured as "Bertie only orders the gold plate when he's well pleased with his guests".

We arrived back in Chicago little dreaming that our innocent excursion which had been prompted only by a very Scottish interest in genealogy, would set a hornets' nest about our ears.

It afterwards transpired that one of our Scottish news-papers, being desirous for news of the Scottish mission in America had cabled the Press Association asking for a story on our progress. Their representative in Chicago, not being able to find us at our hotel had diligently traced our movements throughout that Sunday and had jumped to his own conclusions. The story which appeared in the Press next day described me as having made my headquarters in America in the country home of Colonel "Bertie" McCor-mick and gave it to be understood that my sole purpose was to stir up trouble for England and to emulate the former activities of De Valera among the American Irish.

When I returned to New York I learned that Eric Link-later had immediately and somewhat pompously written to the Editor of the *Scotsman* roundly condemning me for having any truck with such as Colonel McCormick and solemnly withdrawing his signature to the Covenant. By the time I reached Scotland several others, whose allegiance had never been very strong in any case, had followed Linklater's example but whenever I was able to defend myself the trouble soon blew over.

I still do not understand why the trouble should ever have arisen. Two years previously the same Colonel McCormick had visited Glasgow and had been given a civic reception and a luncheon in the City Chambers by the Labour Lord Provost of that time. The same people who condemned me would have been delighted to receive an invitation to that lunch! No one imagined that Scotland had developed violent Anglophobia because of it and if no Scot dare ever speak to any American who has ventured to voice criticism of England we should never meet any American at all!

CHAPTER TWENTY-THREE

Shortly before I had set out for America I had received a delegation of students from Glasgow University who had pressed me to accept nomination as Covenant candidate in the Rectorial Election which was due to take place in October that year. The Covenant Committee and Scottish Convention which still sponsored it, were firmly opposed to the idea of fighting Parliamentary elections but the Rectorial was something different and if we could bring off a victory there it would be of considerable importance in impressing the political parties with our growing strength, especially among the younger members of the community.

On the other hand the candidates already in the field would be formidable opponents. There were Sir David Maxwell Fyfe for the Tories, Dr. George Macleod for the Labour Party and the late Lord Inverchapel as an independent. However, I had decided to fight and had accepted nomination and now that I was back in Scotland I was soon engaged in the activities which are the prelude to such a contest.

It is a well-established tradition that candidates in a rectorial election must not themselves take an openly active part in their campaign but they are expected to advise their followers and they are usually consulted about the policies which should be pursued. Since my home happens to be in the heart of the student quarter in Glasgow I was all too readily accessible both for advice and consultation and from the opening of the University session until polling day I was liable to receive student visitors at almost any hour of the night.

Fortunately for me, the University Covenant Committee which had been brought together to run my campaign numbered among its members many of the most prominent students of their day. They included Bill Craig, President of the Union; Provan Murray, Editor of the *University Magazine;* Jimmy Halliday and Douglas Taylor, Presidents respectively of the Nationalist and Liberal Clubs; and, perhaps most memorable of all, Ian R. Hamilton, a rebellious but brilliant student who had for some time run his own highly critical magazine under the name of *Girn* until the Senate had suppressed it and who was now acting as editor of Covenant literature in the Rectorial campaign.

They were all first-rate fellows and excellent company so that their frequent visits were anything but a burden to me. Most of them had seen active service during the war and they were, therefore, older and more experienced than the usual run of students. They were completely genuine in their support of the Covenant cause and with their enthusiasm and audacity they were able to build up such a campaign as probably had never been seen before. They thought nothing of arranging such pranks as purloining a monkey cage from the Zoo, locking up the President of the Tory Club in it and publicly feeding him with buns in George Square. A day or two before the poll Churchill sent a message in support of Maxwell Fyfe and my committee learned that it was to be published in the Tory magazine under a banner headline "Churchill says vote for Fyfe". The printers' offices were raided, the entire stock of Tory magazines was stolen, and on the next day they were circulated in the University with a huge overprint in red ink so that they read, "Churchill says vote for MacCormick."

Such exploits are, of course, in the true tradition of rectorial elections, but what was really exceptional in the campaign run by my committee was the high quality and sparkling wit of our election newspaper the *Blue Bunnet* produced by Ian Hamilton. Naturally, his editorship involved frequent consultations with me and a close friendship developed between us. Our talks ranged far beyond the immediate business in hand and I remember that on one occasion Ian, who, like most young men, was impatient for action, suddenly exclaimed:

"We must do something dramatic; something which will call the attention of the whole world to our movement!"

I pointed out that we were precluded, by our own resolve never to resort to violence, from doing anything which would endanger anyone's life.

"I agree with that," he said. "But surely there's something we can do which will hurt no one yet make the Government in London a laughing-stock. Politicians will be even more sensitive to ridicule than to violence. Something like taking the Stone of Destiny back to Scotland."

"The idea has often been talked about," I said. "When I was a student myself we even had a plan worked out, but it came to nothing."

Ian laughed. "I've been thinking about it myself for a long time and I'm certain I could do it."

Then we returned to the correcting of proofs and plans for the next issue of the *Blue Bunnet*. But what had been said remained almost tangibly in the air and I knew that I had not heard the last of it.

Voting in the Rectorial Election took place on the morning of Saturday, 21st October, and the result was expected to be announced by one o'clock that day. Throughout the forenoon I tried to carry out my normal office routine without displaying any feeling of excitement. But, in fact, I was secretly wrought up to a high pitch of anxiety. Even some members of the National Covenant Committee had strongly advised against my candidature and I knew that if I were badly beaten the result would be hailed on all sides as a token that the movement had lost its impetus. For many years the Rectorial Election in Glasgow, despite the fact that the franchise was open only to undergraduates who often demonstrated their loyalties in highly unorthodox fashion, was regarded as a kind of political barometer, or rather as an oracle prophesying the mood of the next generation of Parliamentary electors. My success, if I should have any, would no doubt be explained away but my failure would be regarded as a fatal blow to the Covenant.

With these thoughts in my mind I soon became convinced that abject failure was inevitable, and actually brought myself to feel that I was no longer interested in the details of the result. Shortly after midday I left the office and sauntered round to the Art Club where I thought to have a quiet drink before going home to learn the worst. The only other occupant of the Club was none other than a leading member of the University Court—the late John Dunlop Anderson. He greeted me jauntily and told me that he was waiting for a telephone call from the University to tell him the result.

"I'll be the first man to congratulate the new Lord Rector," he declared, "and the first to get a drink for him."

Although I knew and liked Dunlop Anderson I had no idea that his sympathies lay in my direction, and, in my present defeatist mood, I looked at him with a jaundiced eye, convinced that he was merely getting ready to gloat over my discomfiture. However, I did my best to joke with him but when, in a few minutes, the telephone bell rang loudly and he disappeared into the kiosk my courage failed me altogether. I slunk out ignominiously, determined to find my solace in some more humble hostelry and to postpone for a little longer the revelation of bad tidings!

It was well after one o'clock before I took my way home,

still ignorant of the result. As I passed the next door to my own a neighbour ran out to shake hands with me.

"I believe you're the new Lord Rector," he said.

"Oh no," I replied. "I'm sure the result's not public yet. You can't have heard the figures."

"Well," he said, "I'm pretty sure of it. About twenty minutes ago, what looked like half the students in the University went tearing up your stair shouting and singing like the very devil. It can only mean that you've won."

For a moment I remained unconvinced but as I mounted the stair to my own top flat I could myself hear the loud revelry of what sounded very like a victory song from my supporters. Sure enough the house was packed with students, most of them still in the outlandish rags in which they had fought the traditional battle outside the University tower, and I could no longer refuse to face up to a win. In the midst of clamour it was borne in to me that I had won in three "nations" out of four and had, besides, a majority of individual votes. Next came the Independent, Lord Inverchapel, and close behind him Maxwell Fyfe. Labour was out of the running altogether. The Covenant had proved its strength among the young men and women of Scotland and all was well.

For the rest of that day my house was in a state of constant hilarious uproar. At one time I counted no less than 140 people crowded round the piano in one room alone. The eager smiles of these young men and women, their spontaneous song, their sheer joy in victory made it one of the most glorious days in my life and made me feel that in their hands and the hands of thousands of others like them all over the country the future of Scotland was assured.

CHAPTER TWENTY-FOUR

O<small>UR SUCCESS IN</small> the Rectorial Election provided a strong fillip to the Covenant campaign all over the country, but, naturally, the first excitement entailed in collecting signatures by many thousands every week was beginning to wane. We were already approaching the 2,000,000 mark but, obviously we could not go on for ever and our actual organisation, dependent wholly as it was on voluntary workers, was scarcely fitted to consolidate the gains which we had made. Moreover, the war in Korea was now in full swing and going badly for the United Nations so that among the more timid of our own Committee members there were several who counselled caution and urged that for a time we should rest on our oars. It was apparent that in spite of our continued success in maintaining public interest in the Home Rule campaign we could not indefinitely maintain the pressure unless we were fortified by some new and dramatic gesture.

For that reason, I awoke on Christmas morning with a feeling of subdued excitement tingling in my veins. At about eleven o'clock I answered a call on the telephone and heard a mildly conspiratorial voice say:

"I've just had a message from London. Our journalist friend there has brought off his scoop."

I managed to suppress the excitement in my voice and the desire to ask questions. "I'm delighted to hear it," I replied as casually as possible. "Thanks for ringing. I'll see you later about it."

That is how I first learned that the Stone of Destiny had been successfully removed from Westminster Abbey. The news was confirmed by the radio bulletin at one o'clock and that afternoon the screaming headlines in Glasgow's evening Press were the heralds of one of the greatest stories ever to astonish the world.

One by one during the next three days the fugitive reivers returned by devious routes to Glasgow. Each safe arrival was duly reported to me and by Wednesday following Christmas Day it became possible for me to meet them all and hear their story at first hand. I confess that I was wildly thrilled by it. It was a story of courage, tenacity and high resolve with a good deal of humour and sheer luck thrown in. Ian Hamilton, who was, of course, the "ringleader" has retold it all with magnificent verve in his book, *No Stone Unturned*, but the first account of it, told as we drove round the streets of Glasgow in Robert Gray's car remains for me a highlight of sheer romance.

I had already, though not without some misgiving, made up my mind as to my proper attitude to the whole affair. Nothing short of betrayal, of which I cannot think that any Scot would have been guilty, could have prevented Ian and his comrades from their attempt. They were not people in the wild and irresponsible fringe of the Nationalist Movement, but good and steady supporters of the Covenant who were impatient with orthodox political methods. If I had turned a deaf ear to them they would perforce have gone elsewhere. Yet, as Chairman of the Covenant Committee I represented a movement which had always insisted upon a reasonable and constitutional approach towards its goal. It could well be that important members of the Committee would strongly condemn the whole idea. The years which I had spent in endeavour to build up a united body of reasonable Scottish opinion might be cast to the winds. But on the whole I concluded that with careful guidance a situation might develop in which Scottish opinion would be more firmly united than ever before and it was already obvious that we had not over-estimated the dramatic effect on the public mind of such an incident.

During its removal from the Coronation Chair the stone had come away in two unequal pieces, one weighing about 3 cwt. and the other a little under 1 cwt. The two parts were still in England, widely separated from each other, and the problem which now confronted us was how to get them safely back to Scotland. It seemed a formidable task. The Scottish Border was being watched night and day by the police. All roads leading from London were check-pointed and even the docks in London and Leith were under close observation. And to make matters worse, the weather was atrocious with deep snow lying on all the Border roads.

On Friday, 30th December, we all met again, this time in Robert Gray's office which we approached separately and by different routes feeling gloriously conspiratorial. No one had yet thought of a foolproof plan for bringing back the major part of the stone and we did not yet know for certain where the smaller part was. Our only knowledge of it was that it had last been seen by Ian Hamilton when he had put it into the boot of a car to be driven away from London by Kay Matheson, heading vaguely in the direction of Oxford. We knew that it must be safe, for we had learned of Kay's return to her home in Inverasdale, but, for reasons of security, we had not made any direct contact with her.

Alan Stuart, who had been one of the raiders, now turned up with his father's car, ready to travel north to confer with Kay. But as we discussed one unsatisfactory plan after another for recovering the main piece of the stone he suddenly lost patience with our careful calculations of risk.

"Let's go south tonight," he exclaimed. "I've got the car and I'm not expected home for a couple of days. The stone's buried in loose earth and if it's left much longer in this weather it may be damaged by frost."

Within an hour they were off on the second lap of their adventure—Ian Hamilton, Alan Stuart, "Neil" and John Jocelyn—ready to defy all the minions of Scotland Yard at a time when every police station in the country was on the look-out for just such an expedition of Glasgow students.

In little more than twenty-four hours they were back in Scotland with the stone. By prearrangement they communicated with Robert Gray and in his car the precious object was taken immediately to a secure place of hiding in central Scotland. With fitting ceremony it was handed over to the man who was to be its custodian for the next three months, and from that time until the final dénouement in Arbroath not one of the original reivers knew where the Stone was hidden and none of them ever asked. Eight days later Ian Hamilton, singlehanded, recovered the smaller piece of stone from England and it too was placed in the same keeping. It was actually on its way across the Border while I was being installed as Lord Rector at one of the stormiest ceremonies ever witnessed in Glasgow. A good many of my student friends expressed surprise that Ian was absent from this great occasion but I put them off by saying he had a cold.

There followed the long weeks of patient police enquiries, when even the help of water-diviners and clairvoyants was sought by Scotland Yard. Then came the first serious leakage of information, and, if I am right in my surmise, it reflected little credit upon the loud-talking extreme fringe of the Nationalist Movement which was noisily attempting to claim credit for the whole affair.

Of course, nearly every newspaper in Scotland suspected that I must know something about the whereabouts of the Stone and I was constantly subjected to intense and often cunning interrogation by dozens of reporters. To them all I answered with perfect truth that I had no idea where it was but gave them no clue that I was in almost daily communication with its keeper. Their enquiries, however, served the useful purpose that I was able to learn from them the progress of the police investigation, for most of them had sources of information not open to any ordinary member of the public.

By the middle of March, 1951, I knew that the police were fairly sure about the identity of the four original reivers and very soon thereafter they showed their hand by a dramatic dash to Inverasdale where Kay Matheson was interrogated for nearly a whole day by Inspector McGrath and an assistant from London. But I also knew that, under no circumstances, could they ever discover the whereabouts of the Stone and that, of course, was their major concern.

I had a strong feeling that soon I would receive something like an official approach with some kind of offer of negotiations and that all I needed to do was wait. On any reasonable terms I was quite willing to negotiate. Already many people in Scotland even among those who were friendly to us, were beginning to show anxiety about the actual safety of the Stone and I realised that if we could not soon bring it to light it might become more of an embarrassment than an advantage to us. News of the King's illness had reached us and we even heard it suggested that the Queen might make a broadcast appeal for the Stone's return. We thought this unlikely, but it was a possibility to be reckoned with and we knew that if any such thing did happen we would lose the sympathy of a large number of Scots folk who had enjoyed the adventure and were delighted at the discomfiture of starched authority in London, but who would turn against us if we carried things too far. We wanted to preserve as wide a unity of feeling in Scotland as possible.

Sure enough, the first approach soon came. Through one of the newspapers I was asked to meet an eminent London Scot who, I had good reason to believe, was in close touch with members of the Government and particularly with the Secretary of State for Scotland. I readily agreed to meet him and when I did he cautiously asked me whether it would be possible for me to learn on what conditions the Stone might be restored. I undertook quite noncommittally to make enquiries, and, on the following day, I met him again and put these propositions before him:

1. The persons who had removed the Stone and those who had custody of it were anxious to bring it to light in a decent and respectful manner.

2. They suggested that the Stone should be placed in St. Giles' Cathedral.

3. They must have a promise in advance that the Stone would not be removed from St. Giles' during an interval long enough to permit of discussions as to its future taking place at a proper level. The time suggested was six months.

These suggestions were well received by my fellow inter-mediary and he undertook to lay them before the members of the Government concerned. Late in the evening of the same day I was informed that the proposals had been well received in the proper quarters and were likely to prove acceptable but that final agreement could not be indicated until after a Cabinet meeting which was due to be held in a few days' time.

I arranged therefore to have a further meeting with my friend in the following week and, meantime, I agreed to make such arrangements as might be necessary to ensure that the Stone would be readily available.

During all the time since Hogmanay the two parts of the Stone had, of course, remained separately packed in strong wooden cases in their hiding-place. My friends and I realised that it would be unwise ever to produce it in its disparate condition or we should be accused of having wantonly broken it, but our problem now was how to go about the necessary repairs. Obviously we could not conduct operations on the Stone of Destiny in any public place!

We were fortunate in that Robert Gray's business was that of a monumental mason and he could, therefore, supply us with a skilled craftsman and all the necessary tools and materials. All that we needed was to find a suitable place to carry out the job in secrecy.

My own house is a top flat with spacious attics in the West End of Glasgow, and, at first, we decided that for want of anywhere better the work should be done there. We were painfully conscious that I might be under observation but the risk had to be taken.

The custodian of the Stone was naturally a party to all our discussions and he arranged to bring first the smaller part of the Stone to my house where I should be waiting to receive it at eight o'clock in the evening. He would have two identical parcels with him, one containing the Stone and the other coal so that if he saw anything suspicious he would deliver the coal and make off elsewhere with the Stone. In the event it was the coal I received.

When he drew up outside my house he saw two uniformed policemen stationed on the pavement and a police car standing at the end of the block. He naturally supposed either that I was about to be arrested or that the police had got some inkling of our plans. As casually as he could he got out of his car, pulled out a heavy box of coal from the back seat and mounted the stair almost hoping that he might be tapped on the shoulder as he went. Coal was in very short supply at the time and it was no very heinous offence for one friend to help another out with an occasional bucketful.

He waited with me only long enough to explain the danger we were in. He had no plan ready for re-disposal of the Stone but if he could get safely away from the door he would soon think of something.

That night was an anxious one for me! We were so near a successful end to our adventure that it would have been a bitter disappointment to be frustrated at the last moment. And at any instant I expected an imperious knock on my door from the arms of the law.

In the morning I learned that there had been a burglary next door and the police activity in Park Quadrant had nothing at all to do with the Stone of Destiny.

Meantime, my friend had driven away, fully convinced that he was being followed. For some time he twisted backwards and forwards on his course through side streets then set off at high speed for the open country in the direction of Kilsyth. He knew a farmer there whose steading was high up in the Kilsyth Hills and absolutely isolated. He had decided to entrust his precious cargo to him though he knew nothing about his political sympathies.

It has always seemed to me that something of the old spirit of the '45 came back to life in Scotland at that time. Without giving any forewarning my friend reached the farmhouse and knocked at the door.

"Good evening, Mr. McGregor," he said. "I've got something very important in my car. Will you look after it for the night?"

"What is it you have?"

"It's the Stone of Destiny!"

"Man, if you're telling me the truth," said the farmer, "I'd count it an honour to guard it with my life."

After very little further explanation the Stone was secreted in the barn under a pile of hay and a password was arranged so that the farmer would know to whom to deliver it the next day.

Although the affair of the police had been a false alarm we now concluded that my house was the wrong place for the work we had to do. Suddenly, however, I remembered a friend of mine whose house was ideally situated on the very outskirts of Glasgow and whose only near neighbour was a golf-course. He was a douce and highly successful business man in Glasgow but long ago he had been at school with me and he had always been a good supporter of the Home Rule cause.

I called him on the telephone at his office in the morning and asked him to have a coffee with me. When we met I told him the whole story and said we wanted to commandeer his house for the week-end. With the same alacrity as the farmer in Kilsyth he agreed, and declared that he would regard his house as being highly honoured if it could give shelter to the Stone on which so many Scottish kings had been crowned. He explained that, in any case, he and his wife were going down to Rothesay for the week-end and we could have the keys of the house for as long as we needed them.

"Would you be willing to take your car out to Kilsyth this afternoon and collect the smaller piece of the Stone?" I asked.

"I'll do anything that's necessary," he answered without hesitation.

Considering that, according to the Press, the police were already hot on the track of the Stone I thought highly both of his patriotism and his courage. If anything should go wrong now he would, in all probability, be arrested and charged with complicity in an affair about which he had known nothing until that moment. I gave him the password for the Kilsyth farmer and left him with the arrangement that

I would meet him at his house at four o'clock in the afternoon and that, meantime, I would explain matters to his wife and make sure she had no objections to the use to which we proposed to put her home. We both took it for granted that she would not object. She was a Gaelic-speaking girl from Skye whose family had often given me hospitality in the old days of my pioneering in the Highlands.

Meantime, Robert Gray had taken his foreman stone-mason into his confidence and had secured that he would be willing to undertake the work of repair, or, at least, to report whether repair was possible.

Everything went according to plan, and by eight o'clock that evening I found myself alone with the mason and the smaller piece of the Stone in the house in the suburbs. My task was to stand guard until I should be relieved by Robert Gray some time during the night.

Together the mason and I examined the Stone. He was an Aberdonian named Ned Manley, a quiet, steady-looking man nearing sixty years of age, with a twinkle of humour in his eye. As his hand moved lovingly over the Stone he looked up at me and said in his rich Aberdeen accent:

"Aye, man, it's been an auld crack in the Stane. It wasna our laddies wha broke it. I doubt na but what the last twa or three kings hae sat on't and it broken—and them nane the wiser!"

Indeed, there was no doubt even to my inexpert eye that the broken surface showed clear evidence of weathering over a long period and even the angle of the break showed that it had been caused by a natural "dry" in the rock. The iron ring and two links by which the Stone had been carried away from Scotland in 1296 were also badly worn and it looked as though even the slightest of rough handling would sever the ring from its link. The fact that it still held showed, if any further evidence was needed, that, in spite of its adventures since Christmas Day, there had been no care-lessness in its treatment.

I asked Ned how he would go about his task, and whether it was possible to make a beginning even before we had the main bit of the Stone, which could not be delivered till the next day. He showed me his plan, which was to drill two holes at an angle to each other into the broken face and into which he would cement two strong metal pins. He would then drill receiving holes in the other broken face and bring the two parts together so that the pins when firmly cemented would join them.

"You needn't worry about it," he said. "It'll be stronger than it was when it was taken from the quarry hundreds of years ago."

Together we carried the Stone into the kitchen and set it on the table. Then I left him to get on with his work and took up my vigil in the front room in case we should be inter-rupted. In a few minutes I heard the loud noise of mallet on steel in rhythmic blows. I had no idea how stone should be drilled but I had imagined some fairly silent whirring instru-ment neatly doing the job. Now I suddenly became alarmed lest with these blows the Stone should be shattered. I went through to Ned and complained but he laughed at me when I said that I thought he was merely going to drill a hole.

"That's just what I'm doing," he said.

"But does it need all that hammering," I asked.

"It's the only way I know to drill a hole," he said. Then he showed me how it was done, by quickly repeated sharp taps with his mallet on the steel drill which all the time he kept turning in his left hand. Already the hole was beginning to form and there was a little pile of small chips and pow-dered stone on the table. Suddenly I had an idea and asked him whether the powdered stone could be used in preparing the cement. He examined it closely and said that it looked like very fine quality sand and should make a very good cement mixture. We therefore kept it carefully and when, on the following day, the whole operation was successfully completed we felt satisfied that we had used the Stone's own material in its repair. Indeed, when the cement had set it was almost impossible to see any crack at all and even at a distance of a few feet the Stone looked as though it had never been broken. It was a perfect job of work of which both Ned and Robert Gray were justifiably proud.

Two days later our London friend returned to Glasgow and I met him late in the evening in the Central Hotel. Whenever I saw his face I knew he was the bearer of bad news. He told me that the Cabinet had utterly rejected my proposals. The best he could now hope for was that if we returned the Stone to the police we *might* get an undertaking that there would be no prosecutions.

I said that we were not interested in any such undertaking and that in no circumstances would we hand the Stone to the police. I was sorry that the Government had failed to show either generosity or imagination and that an opportunity of demonstrating a real degree of friendship between the English and Scottish peoples had been lost.

Next day I reported again to my friends. The house in the suburbs was no longer a safe hiding-place and once again the Stone must go on its travels.

CHAPTER TWENTY-FIVE

Owing to the turn which events had taken it was thought wise once again that I should not know the new hiding-place of the Stone and, on this occasion, we entrusted the task of finding a safe refuge for it to our old colleague John McNicol. I learned afterwards that he had taken it to Killearn to the house of a friend who, although he was privately sympathetic to our movement, was not a known supporter. There the Stone was completely bricked-in among the foundations of the house and, if we had not again voluntarily moved it, it could have remained safely there to this day and long after. One of the Glasgow C.I.D. officers who had worked on the case along with the Scotland Yard men laughingly told me long after the Stone had been taken back to London that they had just been on the point of discovering it when matters came to a head. In fact, however, neither he nor any other police officer had the slightest clue as to its whereabouts and even I did not know the identity of the new custodian. The reivers themselves, although they had been consulted about everything which was being done, were completely ignorant about the Stone's movements and did not even know that it had been repaired. Even under the most rigorous third-degree examination they could not have given a hint of its hiding-place.

Indeed, throughout all these weeks they had been under considerable nervous strain. They had all been named in the Press as "persons interviewed by the police". They were much more than suspects, and very naturally they were besieged by the Press for interviews and personal stories. They were, moreover, being "played" by the authorities

much as a mouse is played by a cat. Day after day contradic-
tory rumours about imminent arrests were put out from
Scotland Yard or elsewhere. It was a war of nerves in which
all the weapons were on the side of the Government. None
the less, while they were all anxious to bring the affair to an
honourable conclusion, they stood their ground and showed
no sign of breaking down under the strain. Although there
was good reason to believe that the police had a substantial
case against three of them, the fourth, Ian Hamilton, had
never admitted his part in the adventure and it was doubtful
whether, without an admission on his own part and without
any evidence implicating him from the other three, the police
could build up more than a flimsy case against him.

It was at this juncture that a letter appeared in the
Scotsman from Lord Belhaven asking that the Countess of
Erroll, as Lord High Constable of Scotland, should accept
possession of the Stone pending any direction which the King
might give as to its ultimate disposal.

In this letter all of us who were concerned saw an opportunity to open discussions which might both unite public
opinion in Scotland and secure that the Stone would
ultimately be restored to the Scottish people in a proper and
public manner. The opinion of leading Churchmen, advocates and friendly newspaper editors was sought by Covenant
officials in Edinburgh and all were agreed that the Stone
should be publicly brought to light in some suitable place
and that, if this were done, the whole weight of Scottish
sentiment would be behind the claim that the Stone should
be given a permanent home in Scotland.

Lady Erroll was herself consulted and she agreed to issue
an appeal that the Stone should be handed over to the
Church of Scotland authorities. As one of the highest representatives of the Crown in Scotland and as a patriotic
Scotswoman, she was in an invidious position. Her ready

agreement to issue such an appeal was proof at once of her courage and of her appreciation of the historic significance of her high office as Constable of Scotland.

Late on the night of Friday, 6th April, 1951, following upon all these contacts and discussions, a delegation from Edinburgh consisting of Wilfred Taylor of the *Scotsman* and Nigel Tranter, Vice-Chairman of the Covenant Committee, called on me to report and to make proposals. I learned then beyond any reasonable doubt that if the Stone were produced in public, accompanied by appropriate messages both to the King and to the Assembly of the Church of Scotland, we could be assured of the support of the great body of responsible Scottish opinion. It was, indeed, the opportunity for which we had waited—the opportunity to secure that Scotland would speak with a united voice.

We then discussed the choice of a proper place for the dénouement. St. Giles' in Edinburgh was ruled out for we had learned that the police were keeping constant vigil over it. On one occasion even the organist had been arrested and held for questioning after a late evening practice!

Finally, two places emerged from our talks as being suitable—Dunfermline Abbey, the burial-place of Robert Bruce, or the Abbey of Arbroath, scene of the signing of Scotland's Declaration of Independence in the year 1320. There was no difficulty in choosing between these two places. Arbroath was the right place, both in terms of history and of sentiment.

I promised my friends from Edinburgh that I would consult all the people involved and would advise them to deliver the Stone in Arbroath Abbey during the incoming week.

I felt assured in my own mind that whether the Stone were allowed to rest there until it might be transferred to St. Giles or some other suitable church, or whether the police would snatch it unceremoniously away our purpose would be served. In the event, it was the latter course which was followed by the authorities and nothing could more signally have served to awaken the Scottish people to a real sense of their present helplessness as a nation. My friends left me to return to Edinburgh well after midnight, but, unknown to them, another meeting had meantime been gathering in another room in my house. It was a meeting of the then custodians of the Stone and of two of the principal reivers. I reported my conversations fully to them and after some talk, and a careful appraisal of all the possible consequences the Arbroath idea was approved.

In flat contradiction to various rumours which have been put around by ill-disposed persons, no pressure was brought to bear upon us from any quarter whatever and no bargain, whether of immunity from prosecution or otherwise, was made with the Government or any representative of it. Our decision was made solely with regard to the best advantage for the Scottish cause. We saw the Stone, not as an object of superstitious awe, but as a symbolic instrument to remind a whole people of their nationhood It is not in material things, however great their real or their sentimental value, but in the minds of men that destiny is fulfilled.

We had taken the decision but it still remained to carry it out, and that was no easy task. The police were more vigilant than ever. In several interviews to the Press I had publicly commended Lady Erroll's appeal and no doubt those in authority would draw the conclusion that a climax was at hand. Nothing would suit them better than that they should nip our schemes in the bud, and, by a red-handed arrest, bring ridicule upon us. We must work, therefore, in an atmosphere almost of exaggerated secrecy. We dared not use telephones to make contacts nor, as one important experience had taught us, trust any message through the post.

On Monday, 9th April, one of our number went to Arbroath to spy the land and to seek the help of friends there.

The man chosen was that same student "Neil" whose name has never been divulged but who, from the very beginning, had played a leading part in the affair. He is a man of subtle mind, tactful and diplomatic and I knew he could be depended upon to discover the sympathies of those to whom he was sent before disclosing even by a hint the purpose of his visit.

He returned to Glasgow the next day and reported the complete success of his mission. The two leading members of Scottish Convention in Arbroath had proved themselves entirely sympathetic and had readily agreed to help in the fulfilment of our plan. They were in a good position to do so since both of them were highly respected Town Councillors and both were accustomed to playing a prominent part in the annual pageant of Arbroath. They thus had ready access to the Abbey.

There was only one snag. The plan must be carried out the next day for on no other day that week could they be available to help. Arrangements must, therefore, be made at short notice for the collection of the Stone from its hiding-place and for its transport to Arbroath the next morning.

A further meeting of conspirators was summoned at 5 p.m. that afternoon. The time schedule worked out in Arbroath was placed before them. To the credit of all concerned there was no hesitation. If the job must be done tomorrow it would be done. Robert Gray, Ian Hamilton and the anonymous student were selected at their own request to be the bearers of the Stone. In case they might be followed Gray was to go alone to the hiding-place and with the help of the custodians there to load the Stone into the boot of a borrowed car. The two younger men were to go by bus or train to Stirling and were there to thumb a lift from Gray at 10 a.m. on the railway bridge between Stirling and Causewayhead. One of our friends in Arbroath was to meet them near

Forfar and guide them to the Abbey of Arbroath where the other would be waiting to receive them. Each stage was timed to a minute and in the event the plan was carried out with only a few seconds' variation in the appointed times.

On Wednesday, 11th April, I had an engagement to speak to the students of St. Andrews University. I left Glasgow by train at 11.10 a.m. for St. Andrews. All the way to Leuchars I wondered how my friends were faring on their hazardous journey. I knew well the risk they were taking and the possibility of arrest leading not so materially to prosecution but to the kind of ridicule which would destroy all the hopes we had of the affair of the Stone. I was well provided with magazines and newspapers but I read not a word.

At Leuchars I changed trains for St. Andrews. A ticket collector came running along the platform calling into each compartment, "The Stone has turned up in the Abbey of Arbroath!"

I heaved a sigh of relief. As ever, my friends had succeeded! Fine friends, dependable men, the stuff of which the new Scotland will be made—men who laugh at planners and organisers but when a task's to be done they know the way!

In a moment or two my compartment was besieged by reporters. Having heard the news they had come from St. Andrews to meet me and to note my reactions. My first response was to ask them for all the news. They told me how three unidentified men had carried the Stone, draped in the flag of Scotland, to the high altar of Arbroath; how within quarter of an hour a police check had been instituted on all roads leading from the town; but how no arrests had been made. The mystery of the Stone's return was as dramatic as the mystery of its disappearance!

What happened afterwards is all within public knowledge. But what is to happen yet? The old Stone, the known seat of kings for more than a thousand years, has travelled back to its imprisonment in the place where Edward put it 700 years ago. Yet, after all these centuries, it has been long enough again in Scotland to play its part in our new history. It has awakened the people whose symbol it is, and they will not now be content until it is with all honour restored to them— not that they pay it any undue reverence in itself but that its return will foreshadow the return to them of their power to rule themselves and to live their life in their own free way.

CHAPTER TWENTY-SIX

THAT THE Scottish people had indeed been stirred by the incident of the Stone was very soon evident. Immediately after the Stone had been taken back to London the Covenant Committee staged public meetings in Edinburgh, Glasgow, Arbroath itself, Aberdeen, Inverness and Fort William, thus making a sweep right round the country in one week. At all of these meetings Ian Hamilton and I spoke and at some of them we were helped also by the other two student reivers, Alan Stuart and Gavin Vernon. Everywhere the audiences were immense and enthusiastic. Even in staid Aberdeen the huge Music Hall was packed to more than capacity and in Inverness more than 2,000 people stood on a bitterly cold night outside the Town Hall to hear the proceedings being relayed from within.

We were by now, of course, long past the stage of actively seeking new signatures for the Covenant. The total collected was well over 2,000,000 and we had no need of more. What we now wanted to do was to create a nation-wide organisation on a permanent basis, which could maintain the pressure of public opinion even when excitement had died down and the inevitable period of recession should come. All great movements of the people seem to progress in waves, as though there is a deep system of pulsation in human life. The important thing for us to do while we are on the crest of achievement is to prepare our strength and reinforce our resolve so that we are able to survive in the trough and sweep on again to the next summit.

Hitherto the Covenant Movement had not sought to enrol a membership and such organisation as we possessed consisted almost entirely of local committees which had sprung up spontaneously throughout the country for the purpose of gathering signatures. That was no longer enough, and, in June, 1951, after preparing the way by setting up more permanent committees all over Scotland, we combined Scottish Convention and the National Covenant Committee to form the Scottish Covenant Association which is now by far the largest Home Rule organisation in the country and the only one whose declared aim is the establishment of a Scottish Parliament *"within the framework of the United Kingdom."*

The Conservative Government came into power at that time, and, although slowly and unwillingly, it began to show signs of activity in Scotland in response to the pressure of our propaganda. An additional Minister of State, with full Cabinet rank, was appointed to assist the Secretary of State for Scotland and a further Parliamentary Under-Secretary of State, making a total of three, was nominated to deal specifically with Scottish agricultural problems. There thus now exists in Scotland a kind of miniature Cabinet, presided over by the Secretary of State and including Ministers who are responsible on a separate Scottish basis, for home affairs, agriculture, housing, health, fisheries, education, and a host of other matters. They are aided by the Lord Advocate and the Solicitor-General for Scotland and they have under their command a large and efficient staff of Civil Servants centred in St. Andrews House in Edinburgh.

In 1952, the Government took one hesitant step further by appointing a Royal Commission to report on "the exercise of the function of Her Majesty's Government in Scotland". The Commission, under the Chairmanship of the Earl of Balfour, who is largely English in blood and has behind him the typical background of the English aristocracy, was not composed of persons likely to make such recommendations as would cause the Government any serious concern. Out of a membership of fifteen, eleven are noted in *Who's Who*, and of that eleven eight were educated in England and one in Ireland. The views of many of them were, as I well knew in advance, hotly opposed to any from of Parliamentary devolution. They included one of the leading Directors of Outrams, whose *Glasgow Herald* had, for years, been almost the only newspaper in Scotland to oppose the Covenant movement root and branch; and Lady Agnes Dollan whom I had known, even in my old I.L.P. days, as a strong antagonist of Home Rule.

In the event, their report was no better than expected. After two years of deliberation they produced a document so strikingly dull, so lacking in imagination, so self-contradictory and inconsistent, and so timid in recommendation that it has actually redounded to the benefit of the Home Rule cause. Even those who would have welcomed a serious attempt at the refutation of our arguments are disappointed and depressed by what looks so obviously a cooked-up report designed merely to keep Scotland quiet and to suit the policies of the two major political parties.

At first, however, it seemed as though the Royal Commission might at least serve the Government's purpose in damping down the enthusiasm which the Covenant campaign had engendered. It was a natural reaction for people on the doubtful side of the fence to say that they would suspend judgement until the Commission had reported. To some extent, therefore, the wind was taken out of our sails and for a time we concentrated on the preparation of a lengthy memorandum of evidence to place before the Commissioners. The memorandum, which is largely the work of two of the leading members of the Covenant Association, Mr. Douglas Neillands, advocate, and Mr. James A. A. Porteous, our economic adviser, has subsequently been published and widely distributed under the title of *The Case for Scottish Devolution.* It is by far the most comprehensive and closely reasoned statement of the argument for Scottish Home Rule which has ever appeared, and, beside it, the actual report of the Royal Commission seems painfully weak and slap-dash. We thought it wise, however, to take no further major step in the development of our policy until the Commission had concluded its task.

But, in the meantime, an opportunity arose to call attention in a most dramatic manner to the constitutional safeguards which ought to preserve something at least of the identity of Scotland. On the death of King George VI Her present Majesty succeeded to the Throne and was immediately proclaimed under the title of "Elizabeth the Second". Although there is no more loyal part of the Queen's dominions than Scotland the proclamation was received here with widespread resentment. The former Elizabeth had reigned over England alone and no other queen of that name had ever occupied the throne of the United Kingdom of Great Britain. How then could Her Majesty be described as the second Elizabeth of Great Britain? The assumption in the minds of most Scots was that the numeral could only convey and was deliberately intended by her advisers to convey, that Great Britain was really England continuing and that the Union with Scotland had merely been an annexation of the smaller realm.

It was significant of the new temper in Scotland that several provosts of Scottish towns refused to read the proclamation in its official form and that when, with unnecessary ceremony, a new pillar-box bearing the offending numeral was unveiled in Edinburgh it was promptly blown up. Pillar-boxes in Scotland now bear no numeral and it is, unfortunately, tempting to conclude that violence pays better dividends than reasoned protest!

My own interest in the matter was largely from the legal

and constitutional view. Even as a law student in Glasgow University studying constitutional law and history I had resented and suspected Dicey's famous doctrine of the sovereignty of Parliament, which, of course, we were taught to regard as sacrosanct. Throughout the writings of all the English constitutional lawyers, and particularly those of Professor Dicey, there runs the arrogant assumption that the history of the Kingdom of England has been continuous from the Norman Conquest until the present day. The Treaty of Union which on 1st May, 1707, created, under certain unalterable conditions, the entirely new Kingdom of Great Britain, is represented as being of no more consequence, and no more binding on subsequent Parliaments than any prior act of the English Parliament. Dicey, indeed, went so far as to say specifically that the Act of Union is from the point of view of constitutional law of no greater importance that an Act to govern the practice of the dental profession! Even as recently as 1945, the Speaker of the House of Commons ruled that the Parliament of Great Britain was in fact the Parliament of England and that the rules of procedure established there prior to 1707 were still applicable and binding.

Such views would never stand one moment's examination in any court of international law. That they are entirely without foundation is apparent on the following considerations:

(1) The Treaty of Union, ratified by separate Acts of the Parliaments of England and Scotland, was an instrument of agreement between two sovereign nations and contained a number of clauses which were, in so many words, declared to be either "fundamental and essential conditions of Union in all time coming" or else effective "for ever". The persons who framed and agreed to the Treaty knew perfectly well what they were doing, for many other clauses which dealt with the issues of everyday life were declared to be alterable

in future by the new Parliament of the United Kingdom. There thus existed in their minds a clear distinction between the things that were to endure in all time as utterly binding and the more temporal provisions which circumstance might later alter.

(2) The constitutional history of England and Scotland had been very different right down to the moment of Union. In England the law was the law of conquest. The king, having imposed himself upon the people, could do no wrong. He was above all law and could never be challenged in the Courts which, by his own grace, he had appointed to resolve disputes among his subjects. His ministers were answerable only to himself and any notion that the "community", the conquered and enslaved people of England, had any rights against him, was treasonable to entertain.

Scotland was very different. The country had never been conquered, even by the Romans, and the people still felt themselves to be of the same kith and kin as their kings and rulers. Time and again, in the great moments of their history, it had been the "Community of Scotland" and not the King "by and with the advice of his lords spiritual and temporal and his commons in Parliament assembled", which had proclaimed the truths of nationhood. The feeling of the true power of the people found its expression in the unique "law of desuetude". Under the dispensation of that law, though King and Parliament might make statutes, if they were not obeyed by the commonalty they were no longer binding on the individual. No great lapse of time was necessary thus to invalidate a Statute. What was required, was simply the manifest will of the community to repeal it.[1]

It is obvious that any such notion of law is wholly inconsistent with the doctrine of Parliamentary sovereignty. The

[1]See Green's *Encyclopaedia of Scots Law*, Vol. 14, p. 232, for statement of the law and further references.

Parliament of Scotland, which had always been subject to
the ultimate sanction of community assent, had no sovereign
powers itself and could not, therefore, by the Act of Union
convey sovereign powers to its successor the Parliament of
the United Kingdom. There is a useful Latin tag to describe
the situation—*nemo dat quod non habet* (no one can give what
he has not got)—and the Parliament of Scotland could not
by any conceivable rule of law create a new institution with
powers wider than its own.

It followed, therefore, that the Parliament of Great
Britain could not enjoy any greater powers than the Parliament of Scotland and that, in any case, it was limited by the
"entrenched" clauses in the Treaty which had created it.
Even the English Parliament, by expressly repealing in the
Act of Union all laws inconsistent with its terms must be
held to have surrendered any sovereign powers it may have
possessed.

With these considerations in my mind I proposed to the
National Committee of the Covenant Association that we
should use the question of the Queen's title as an issue in the
supreme Court of Scotland in order to secure a ruling, or, at
least, the expression of an opinion, on these vital matters of
constitutional law. Unfortunately, my suggestion created a
miniature uproar and one or two members of the Committee
went so far as to accuse me, not merely of defective judgement but of downright disloyalty. I could have forced the
issue, for the majority clearly understood my purposes, but,
out of deference to the minority, I agreed to postpone any
further action. None the less, one or two of our members
resigned and made some fuss in the Press in doing so. They
were, most of them, people who had been attracted to the
movement by its sudden leap into public prominence and
while I deplored their defection I did not feel that it was
a mortal blow to our cause.

In 1953, shortly before the time appointed for the Coronation, Parliament passed the Royal Style and Titles Act. I thought I saw some fundamental weaknesses in that Act and that they might be useful in the kind of argument which I still had in mind. I consulted Ian Hamilton, who was now studying for the Scottish Bar, and John Bayne, one of our most active members who was also a busy advocate. They agreed with what I had to say and between us we drew up an action of interdict in which we asked the Court of Session to pronounce an order prohibiting Her Majesty's ministers from describing her as the "Second" of Great Britain. No such action had ever been framed before, and since we, therefore, lacked all precedent we had grave doubts as to whether we should even get past the Bill Chamber. Nevertheless, we persevered and finally our case was enrolled under the names of MacCormick and Hamilton *v*. the Lord Advocate. Ian and I had decided to raise the action in our own names so that, if we were ignominiously thrown out of Court before our argument was stated, the Covenant Committee could repudiate us if it wished. We arranged that John Bayne should act as counsel for Ian and that, as one of the parties to the action, I should speak for myself.

With surprisingly little difficulty and almost to our own surprise, we got over the first hurdle in the Bill Chamber where the Crown took objection to the relevancy of our pleadings. Lord Sorn there held that at least we had stated our case competently enough to justify an issue and, in due course, we appeared before Lord Guthrie in the Outer House of the Court of Session to debate our pleas. It was exactly three days before the Coronation and inevitably an immense public interest was aroused. Before a packed Courtroom we argued our pleas against Dicey and the accepted view of the Constitution and protested that the Royal Style and Titles Act of 1953 could have no validity.

Lord Guthrie listened to us somewhat stolidly and seldom interrupted us. From this lack of interruption I knew that he felt little real interest in the argument and that so far as he was concerned our case would be emphatically dismissed. On the following day he delivered his judgement and completely overruled everything we had said. He declared that Dicey had been accepted for several generations in all our law schools in Scotland as *the* authority on the Constitution and implied that it was rather ridiculous for us now to challenge him. He subscribed fully to the doctrine of Parliamentary sovereignty and paid no attention to our claim that, in any case, the Act of 1953 was unintelligible. It was as complete a defeat as I could possibly have feared, with not one word of comfort in his findings.

The only thing which could be said in our favour was that at least Lord Guthrie had treated us seriously and had thought it necessary to pronounce a lengthy opinion to justify the rejection of our contentions. We took enough hope from that small encouragement to intimate an appeal to the Inner House of the Court of Session.

Perhaps a word here about procedure in our Scottish Courts may not be out of place. Even the Scots people themselves are nowadays sadly ignorant about their own legal forms and confuse them with those of England. It is one of the effects of the circulation of a so-called "national" Press, emanating from London, that many people in Scotland think we have such absurd anachronisms as coroner's enquiries, decrees *nisi* in divorce actions, and re-trials when our juries are not unanimous!

The Court of Session, which was established as a College of Justice more or less in its present form in 1454, consists of fourteen Senators or Judges. Of these, six are called Lords Ordinary, who act as judges of the first instance and who sit in what is called the Outer House. The word "outer" has now no positional significance but it is a relic of the days when the Court sat in the old Tolbooth or Town House of Edinburgh and there was, in fact, an Outer House, or kind of lodge, in which the junior judges sat, and an Inner House in which their seniors met as Courts of Appeal.

In the Inner House there are two divisions known as the first and second division and respectively presided over by the Lord President and the Lord Justice Clerk. On each division there are four judges (of whom three are a quorum) and their jurisdiction is identical. In cases of very great moment or difficulty the whole College of Senators may sit together and act as a kind of Grand Jury of the Realm.

The Appeal which we now took to the Inner House could go either to the First or Second Division but we very much hoped that in the luck of the draw we should find ourselves in the First Division. Lord President Cooper would there be the presiding judge and it is no disparagement of any other Senator of the College of Justice to say that he is one of the most distinguished jurists who has ever held that high position. He has, moreover, for many years taken a profound and scholarly interest in the history of the law of Scotland and we knew that on more than one occasion he had called the attention of learned societies to some of the distinctive features of the law of the Scottish constitution. We ventured to hope that if we could state our case before a Bench on which he presided we could be assured that our pleadings would be fully understood if not upheld.

In due course our Appeal was put out for hearing early in July, 1953, and we learned with satisfaction that the First Division was to take it. Both John Bayne and myself prepared ourselves to such a pitch that we thought we could answer any conceivable question from the Bench and go down fighting to the end. We had not the slightest expectation that the Court would now pronounce against the

Queen's numeral but we hoped against hope that something might emerge which would shake the monstrous notion that the Parliament of Great Britain was simply the Parliament of England to which a handful of Scottish members had been added. We prepared all our arguments with a view to eliciting at least a statement of opinion on that all-important question.

I must admit that when the day came for the hearing I was in a state of acute depression and nervousness. Many of our best friends had thought it unwise to pursue the matter to such lengths and advice had not been wanting to the effect that we should just make fools of ourselves in the Inner House. I had practised the law for more than twenty years, but only as a solicitor, and I was unaccustomed even to speaking in the lower Courts. Now I was to advance a thesis which had been dear to my mind from student days but which might seem in the cold light of other people's reason to be merely a wild bee in my bonnet.

When I arrived in the Court I derived not a little comfort from the presence of John Bayne, bewigged and gowned as an advocate should be. To him, although the case was important, appearance in Court was an everyday business, and, win or lose, one could only do one's best. He sensed my nervousness and volunteered to speak first although, as the only counsel engaged, he was properly entitled to the last word for our side.

The Courtroom was crowded. Not only had a large representation of the general public turned out but also every advocate who had time on his hands squeezed in to hear the fun. The argument lasted all day. John Bayne spoke for more than an hour and then I was on my feet for at least two hours. Unlike Lord Guthrie, all three judges on the Bench, and particularly the Lord President continually interrupted us, seeking to follow every point to its logical conclusion. We had been wise to be well prepared, for we were subjected almost to a cross-examination from the Bench. I was certainly not displeased. In the give and take of argument every vestige of nervousness disappeared and I found myself at long last proclaiming in public in the Supreme Court of Scotland the disagreement with Dicey which long ago as a student I had longed to express to my mentors. When the hearing ended we were surrounded by congratulatory crowds and one eminent Q.C. in the enthusiasm of the moment went so far as to predict a complete victory for our side.

That, of course, was too good to be true. Three weeks later the Court issued its judgement and upheld the findings of Lord Guthrie. But they did so for very different reasons from his and in a long accompanying opinion[1] the Lord President gave the full support of his authority for the most vital of our arguments. He rejected the view that the Constitutional Law of England automatically became the law of Scotland after the Union; he agreed that the Royal Titles Act was incapable of judicial interpretation and that there was, therefore, no Parliamentary authority for the use of the numeral in the Queen's title; he declared that the doctrine of the sovereignty of Parliament had no counterpart in the law of Scotland and that the Act of Union could not in its fundamental clauses be altered at will by the Parliament of Great Britain; and, perhaps best of all, by reserving his opinion on the right of the Court of Session in certain circumstances to quarrel with Parliamentary legislation he left the door open for future action when a suitable occasion arises. We were naturally jubilant. The law could never again be stated in Scottish textbooks as though Scotland were a mere appendage of England[2] and we had been fully

[1] See Appendix Three.
[2] See *Scottish Juridical Review*, February, 1954.

justified in persisting with our case. The final satisfaction came weeks later when the Crown applied in Court for an award of the expenses of the Appeal. The Lord President refused the application on the ground that we had acted in a representative capacity in a matter of great public interest.

CHAPTER TWENTY-SEVEN

I HAVE TAKEN THE story of Scotland's modern reawakening right down to the present time. As I write these words in November, 1954, I am approaching in a few days my own fiftieth birthday. During the whole of my adult life I have been completely immersed in the National Movement and while I cannot therefore be wholly objective in my judgements, I believe that many others will agree with me when I say that, in the past thirty years, there has been a remarkable change in the whole life of Scotland and in the outlook of the Scottish people.

In the nineteen-twenties the spirit of the people, crushed by economic disaster, lay dormant. But the nation which had endured against all odds for nearly two thousand years was not dead, and among men and women of my own generation it seemed that suddenly once again the spirit began to move.

We are still far from our ultimate goal of a free Scotland in a Federal United Kingdom, but much has been achieved. In 1927, the affairs of Scotland were in the charge of the Scottish Secretary who occupied a mean and indeterminate place in the ministerial hierarchy and whose work was wholly carried on from Whitehall. Today we have both a Secretary of State and a Minister of State of full Cabinet rank and, as I have already pointed out, almost the whole machinery of Scottish administration centred in Edinburgh. The North of Scotland Hydro-Electric Board, under the Chairmanship of Thomas Johnston, is hard at work transforming the face of the Highlands and harnessing the power which Nature has given us. A host of voluntary non-political organisations, with the Scottish Council (Development and Industry) in the lead are building up the Scottish economy and achieving fine results in advertising Scottish products and making the name of Scotland known abroad. The Edinburgh Festival Society, which has sprung up since the war, has already made Edinburgh once again a cultural capital and in Glasgow the Citizens' Theatre, founded by the late James Bridie (Dr. O. H. Mavor) is actively and successfully promoting Scottish drama.

But it is perhaps in the symbols which men use that their deepest sentiments are most readily expressed. Thirty years ago a Scottish flag was a rarity and was invariably printed in the wrong colours. During the Coronation celebrations in 1953 the saltire and royal blue of St. Andrew flew proudly above nearly every building in Scotland and strangers remarked that it far outnumbered every other flag on display. When the Queen Mother opened the Scottish Industries Exhibition in the Kelvin Hall in Glasgow in September, 1954, the same flag flew from dozens of poles outside the hall and made a lovely show against a fine autumn sky.

Flags as well as straws show the way the wind is blowing. Movements of the spirit, springing from the most deeply rooted sentiments of the people, can never be denied their goal. There is no doubt in my mind that long before the end of this century the Parliament of Scotland will once more be opened with ancient pomp and ceremony and that in this new age the representatives of her people will make her a valued partner in the British Commonwealth and an ideal ground for experiments in human progress. The promise implicit in her long history will yet be fulfilled.

Meantime the struggle goes on. We fight, not against oppression from without, but against the private ambitions and narrow partisanship of our own politicians. It has been a long race but the last lap is now to come.

APPENDIX ONE

THE FOLLOWING PROPOSALS for the establishment of a Scottish Parliament were approved by the Scottish National Assembly on 20th March, 1948, and have since been the basis of the Scottish Covenant campaign:

1. There shall be established in Scotland a Parliament which shall have the final legislative authority in all matters in so far as they affect Scotland, with the exception of those matters enumerated in Schedule A appended hereto, which shall be reserved to the United Kingdom Parliament, and those enumerated in Schedule B, which shall be dealt with partly by each Parliament. Schedule C deals with the matters falling within the exclusive legislative power of the Scottish Parliament. The financial relations between the United Kingdom Government and the Scottish Government shall be on the basis set out in Schedule D.

2. The Scottish Parliament shall consist, in the first instance, of a single chamber which shall be composed of two members elected by each of the constituencies returning members to the Commons House of the United Kingdom Parliament. It shall be in the power of the Scottish Parliament to alter the boundaries and the numbers of the constituencies which shall elect members to the Scottish Parliament, and the franchise for such elections and the mode of election to be adopted.

3. The Scottish Parliament shall have full power to repeal, alter or amend any Act passed by the Scottish Parliament before 1707 or by the United Kingdom Parliament thereafter in so far as affecting Scotland, except in so far as it deals with matters which are reserved to the United Kingdom Parliament.

4. The Scottish Parliament shall have power to alter its own Constitution, but no amendment shall be made to the effect of altering its relationship to the United Kingdom Parliament until any such amendment shall have been considered and approved by a Joint Commission representative of the United Kingdom Parliament and of the Scottish Parliament.

5. During the first two years after the setting up of the Scottish Parliament there shall continue to be sent to represent Scottish interests in the United Kingdom Parliament the number of members who at the time of the establishment of the Scottish Parliament represent Scottish constituencies in that Parliament and sixteen representative peers in the House of Lords in that Parliament. Arrangements shall be made to provide that Scottish representatives in the United Kingdom Parliament shall not take part in any proceedings of Parliament dealing solely with English or Welsh domestic affairs. The position with regard to the representation of Scotland in the United Kingdom Parliament shall be determined thereafter by a Commission set up jointly by the United Kingdom Parliament and the Scottish Parliament.

6. In the event of any dispute arising between the United Kingdom Parliament and the Scottish Parliament as to their respective powers, the matter may be referred for a final decision to the Judicial Committee of the Privy Council.

Schedules

A. *Matters Reserved for the United Kingdom Parliament*

1. Crown and Matters relating thereto:
   - (*a*) Succession.
   - (*b*) Regency.
   - (*c*) Civil List.
2. Peace and War.
3. Defence Services.

4. Foreign Affairs and Extradition.
5. Dominions, Colonies, Overseas Possessions, Protectorates and Mandated Territories.
6. Treason and Alienage.
7. Currency, Coinage, Legal Tender, and Weights and Measures.
8. Electoral Law in so far as affecting the United Kingdom Parliament.

B. *Matters to be dealt with Partly by United Kingdom and Partly by the Scottish Parliament*

1. Postal, Telegraph and Telephone Services, with Submarine Cables and Wireless Telegraphy used in connection therewith.

    Note: The United Kingdom Parliament shall be the general authority in regard to Post Office matters including postal rates, but there shall be set up a Scottish Postal Department for the administration of these services in Scotland. The Scottish Government shall have the power to approve the design and authorise the issue of distinctive stamps for use in Scotland.

2. Lighthouses, Buoys and Beacons.

    Note: The general legislative authority with regard to lighthouses, etc., in Scottish territorial waters shall be the Scottish Parliament; but the Admiralty's requirements will be given effect to.

3. Public Docks and Harbours.

    Note: These are to be administered in the same way as lighthouses, etc.

4. Land Acquisition for Public Purposes.

    Note: All land to be acquired for public purposes by departments of the Scottish Government shall be dealt with solely by the Scottish Parliament and under its control. Where land is required by departments of the United Kingdom Government for matters affecting Scotland which are reserved to the United Kingdom Parliament, the Scottish Parliament shall have the final decision as to what land is to be acquired by them; provided that in time of war, land required for the purposes of defence may be acquired by the appropriate departments of the United Kingdom Government.

5. Corrupt Practices.

  Note: Legislation regarding corrupt practices in election of members of the United Kingdom Parliament shall be the province of that Parliament. In all other cases, such legislation shall be within the province of the Scottish Parliament.

C. *Matters Falling Within the Exclusive Legislative Power of the Scottish Parliament*

1. All matters not mentioned in Schedule A or B.
2. The following are given as illustrations only of the matters to be dealt with by the Scottish Parliament:

  (*a*) Industrial Legislation, including administration of industries already nationalised or publicly controlled.

  (*b*) Agriculture and Land:
    i. Ordnance Survey.
    ii. Forestry.
    iii. Importation and Diseases of Animals.

  (*c*) Commercial Undertakings, Professions, etc.:
    i. Advertising.
    ii. Amusement Places—Theatres, etc.
    iii. Banks and Savings Banks.
    iv. Building Societies, etc.
    v. Markets and Fairs.
    vi. Liquor Licensing, etc.

(*d*) Ecclesiastical Matters.

(*e*) Administration of the Law, Civil and Criminal.

(*f*) Education—Primary, Secondary, University and Technical.

(*g*) Local Government and Municipal Undertakings.

(*h*) Local Legislation.

(*i*) Public Health.

(*j*) Housing.

(*k*) Social Insurance and Security.

(*l*) Crown, etc.
  i. Crown Properties in Scotland.
  ii. Treasure Trove.
  iii. Crown Appointments in Scotland.

(*m*) Fisheries—Sea and Inland.

(*n*) Transport—Land, Sea and Air (including roads and canals).

(*o*) Fuel and Power.

(*p*) Broadcasting.

(*q*) Marriage and Divorce.

(*r*) Registration and Census.

(*s*) Immigration.

(*t*) Food Regulations.

(*u*) Revenue Matters falling within the powers of the Scottish Parliament as more fully set forth in the financial proposals.

(*v*) Scientific and Industrial Research.

D. *Financial Relations*

1. *Joint Exchequer Board*

For the adjustment of financial balances between the Scottish and United Kingdom Governments a joint Exchequer Board shall be established, composed of two representatives of the Scottish Ministry of Finance, two representatives of the United Kingdom Treasury, and an independent Chairman, who shall be chosen jointly by the United Kingdom and the Scottish Governments.

2. *Customs*

The power to levy Customs Duties shall be reserved to the United Kingdom Government.

3. *Excise*

Power to levy Excise Duties on articles manufactured or produced shall be reserved to the United Kingdom Government. All other Excise Duties (including Motor Licence Duties and Licences of all kinds) shall be transferred to the Scottish Government.

4. *Income Tax, Surtax and Other Taxes on Profits*

Power to levy Income Tax, Surtax, and other taxes on Profits shall be transferred to the Scottish Government, the net receipts of the Scottish and United Kingdom Governments under these heads being determined in accordance with paragraph 9 below.

5. *Estate Duties*

Estate Duties shall be transferred to the Scottish Government.

6. *Post Office Revenue*

Post office Revenue shall be allocated on the same basis as revenue from Reserved Taxes.

7. *Broadcasting*

The Revenue from Wireless Licences in Scotland shall be paid to a Scottish Broadcasting Corporation.

8. *Allocation of Revenue from Reserved Taxes*

The allocation to Scotland of revenue from Reserved Taxes shall be determined by the following method. The Scottish contribution to Estate Duties during the immediately preceding seven years, expressed as a percentage of total British receipts shall be taken as a basic rate for the purposes of calculation, and to this basic rate there shall be added $2\frac{1}{2}$ per cent. of total British receipts from Reserved Taxes during the Financial Year.

9. *Revenue from Income Tax, Surtax and Taxes on Profits*

The Inland Revenue machinery for collecting these taxes shall continue to be administered as a United Kingdom service. The Scottish share of Revenue from these taxes shall be determined as follows:

(*a*) If the rate of tax were the same in Scotland and England, the basic rate applicable to revenue from Reserved Taxes would apply also to revenue from taxes on income and profits, with the addition of $2\frac{1}{2}$ per cent. of total British receipts from the latter during the Financial Year.

(*b*) If the rate of tax were higher or lower in Scotland, the amount due would first be calculated as if the rate of taxation were the same, and the resulting figures would then be adjusted in proportion to the difference in the effective rate of taxation.

10. *Unemployment*

United Kingdom control of Customs, the major Excise Duties, Defence and Foreign Policy, involves a United Kingdom responsibility for the maintenance of full employment and for meeting the consequence of any unemployment that may occur.

An adjustment shall, therefore, be made in respect of any expenditure in connection with unemployment, such as to equalise the burden throughout the United Kingdom.

The basis of calculation shall be the number of insured workers in Scotland and Great Britain respectively, and the total cost of Unemployment Benefit, Assistance, or other similar measures of relief in the whole of Great Britain shall be borne in this ratio, regardless of the actual local incidence of unemployment.

11. *Special Excise Adjustment*

There shall be added 15 per cent. of total receipts from the duty on whisky to the Scottish share of receipts from the duty as determined under the terms of paragraph 8.

12. *Imperial Contribution*

An Imperial Contribution shall be payable by Scotland in respect of the cost of services reserved to the United Kingdom Government and of the United Kingdom National Debt. The amount of the Imperial Contribution payable by Scotland shall be determined by the Joint Exchequer Board, on the following basis:

Subject to the provisos hereunder the total net revenue of Scotland (i.e. the product of transferred taxes and any non-tax revenue pertaining directly to the Scottish Government plus the residuary share of reserve taxes) shall be determined by the Joint Exchequer Board being such amount as is necessary to cover the cost of administration and services in Scotland at a standard corresponding to that prevailing in England. To the extent that the total gross revenue of Scotland (i.e. including the whole revenue attributable to Scotland from reserved taxes and other taxes collected on a United Kingdom basis) exceeds the necessary expenditure the balance available shall determine the Imperial Contribution.

The provisos above referred to are:—

i. In assessing the total of necessary Scottish Expenditure the Joint Exchequer Board shall be required to make due allowance for the necessary priority of local needs.

ii. Where the rate of taxation in Scotland is lower or higher than in England the amount of the Imperial Contribution shall be calculated as if the rate were the same.

iii. The amount of the Imperial Contribution shall not bear a greater proportion to the contribution of England to Imperial Expenditure than the ratio of taxable income in Scotland to taxable income in England.

APPENDIX TWO

(a) Leading Article published in the Economist *on 8th July, 1950*

IT IS EASY TO forget that the British are not a homogeneous race and that the island which they inhabit is one political entity only because the political independence of two of its three races has been extinguished. For many years it was assumed that—whatever trouble the Irish might create—the political status of Wales had been irrevocably settled in the Middle Ages, and that the relation of Scotland and England had been fixed for ever by the Act of Union. A generation ago this view went almost unchallenged except by a few romantic idealists such as Cunninghame Graham, for Macaulay had educated public opinion to believe in the perfection of existing constitutional arrangements, and in any case the government at Westminster dealt very gently with the liberties of both local institutions and of individuals.

But with the growth of centralised planning and the enormous expansion of the powers of the departments in Whitehall, there has been a growing demand in both Scotland and Wales for a greater measure of local autonomy than is granted at present. Last Saturday Lady Megan Lloyd George, the Deputy Leader of the Liberal Party, moved at a meeting in Llandrindod Wells, which included many of the leading figures in Welsh life, a resolution for parliamentary self-government for Wales. In Scotland the demand for home rule has since the war taken the form of support for the Scottish Convention, an ably led body which seeks the limited aim of a Scottish Parliament with powers over domestic subjects. This organisation has so far secured about a million and a quarter signatures, or just under half the voting turnout in Scotland at the last general election. This week the appointment of a departmental committee under the chairmanship of Lord Catto, the late Governor of the Bank of England, to study the Anglo-Scottish statistics has been announced. It is to be presumed that this committee will provide the groundwork for an official answer to the contention of the Scottish Convention that Scotland contributes more to the revenue of the United Kingdom than it receives back in benefits and services.

The record of official action during the past few years shows that the Government has responded up to a point, to the pressure of Scottish and Welsh opinion for greater freedom and administrative autonomy. Since the end of the war an annual White Paper on Welsh affairs has been published. In 1948 the Government, though rejecting the proposal to create a Secretary of State for Wales, set up an advisory council for Wales and Monmouthshire. The concessions to Scottish national pride have been more extensive. Just before the war the administrative centre of the Scottish Office was removed from London to Edinburgh. In 1948 the Government strengthened the position of the Scottish Grand Committee of the House of Commons by enabling it to debate Scottish Bills in principle. But any proposals for effective home rule—that is, for the creation of a Scottish or Welsh Parliament with control over domestic policy and expenditure—still meets with stony opposition in Whitehall.

It would be difficult to say exactly what it is that inspires the present demand in Wales and in Scotland for a greater measure of political freedom. National pride, the memory of old achievements and ancient wrongs, the wish to preserve Celtic culture, the desire to arrest London's slow drain of all vitality and strength, or a sheer anarchic dislike of strong government—all these play an important part in the minds of the leaders of the movements. But it is fair to say that the support which they have begun to acquire among ordinary people is due to the growing centralisation of all power and decision in hands of the Government of the United Kingdom and its servants. The utilitarian arguments for home rule are becoming more cogent in Scotland and Wales as it becomes increasingly difficult to exercise any local initiative or take any important action without reference to Whitehall.

Thus what the leaders of the Welsh and Scottish home rule movements now demand is the very thing which the officials of Whitehall have persuaded generations of politicians to oppose—the hiving off of control from the central to local governments. To suggest that the Civil Service consciously sees its power threatened by demands for home rule, and constantly uses its influence with Ministers to oppose it, would be to paint too melodramatic a picture. The fact nevertheless remains that politicians, and whole parties, who are sympathetic to home rule when in opposition, find that it is not expedient to do anything about it when they are in office. Just what the arguments are that are whispered so potently in Whitehall, but which cannot be repeated in public, it is really very difficult to say. One suspects that it is not so much deliberate power-seeking as misplaced paternalism, a reflection of the growing belief that people cannot be trusted to decide things for themselves. They may be right; Scottish and Welsh governments might make a lot of mistakes. But what the official mind does not realise is that this is not by a long chalk a decisive argument. The Scots and Welsh have a right to govern themselves foolishly if they wish, and if it will do no great harm to their neighbours.

Private and public opinion in England, as distinct from the official view, so far as it can be ascertained does not seem to share this hostility to the principle of home rule. Most of the factors that bedevilled and long delayed the grant of home rule to Ireland do not apply either to Scotland or Wales; and as for those that do exist, the Irish case has taught the English their lesson. Ireland has also proved, in the constitution of Northern Ireland, that it is perfectly possible to devise a system that provides substantial home rule without disrupting the basic structure of the United Kingdom. To the proposition that the Scots and the Welsh, if they can prove themselves reasonably united in the demand, should have home rule on the Northern Ireland pattern, there would probably be an overwhelming majority of assent among the English public.

The essential proviso, of course, is that the transfer of powers should not be such as to endanger the safety of the realm, to weaken it in its external relationships or to undermine its wealth or welfare. All these, however, are safeguarded under the constitution of Northern Ireland, where the writ of the United Kingdom still runs.

(b) *Leading Article published in the* Scotsman *on 5th August, 1950*

Mr. Hector McNeil, Secretary of State for Scotland, has given the National Covenant Committee the "brush-off". He has told them that in the Government's view "constitutional change in this country is considered and settled by the normal processes of Parliamentary democracy". The Government, of course, do not want to deal with the question of Scottish devolution and are therefore temporising. They cannot be brought to say what evidence would satisfy them that the people of Scotland desired the establishment of a Scottish Parliament within the framework of the United Kingdom or to agree that such a Parliament should be instituted if satisfactory evidence of such a desire were produced. They have already had two indications of this desire —first, the sample plebiscite at Kirriemuir and, secondly, the number of signatures secured for the Covenant—but their attitude is that a Scottish Parliament could be instituted only if there was a majority in favour of it in the British Parliament. It is an invitation to Scotsmen to make their weight felt, but it is issued in the comfortable conviction that Scottish devolution could never become the overriding question at a British General Election. Scotland might be driven to rally to such a cause, but England obviously would not. The Government's attitude is almost an invitation to copy the example of Ireland, and by obstruction, if not worse, to force upon Parliament the necessity of facing the question.

Of the signatories of the Covenant the great majority are moderate-minded men. They recognise that in a General Election Scottish devolution should not be the main issue, but they do not see why the question should be shelved. There ought to be some means within the structure of the United Kingdom of dealing with such a problem as this, and they know, of course, that it has been dealt with in Northern Ireland. Mr. McNeil is averse to a plebiscite, but the Labour Government insisted in March, 1948, that confederation with Canada should be one of the issues set before the people of Newfoundland at the referendum held in June. It suits the present Government, however, to emphasise the imperfections of a plebiscite as a means of ascertaining public opinion. These imperfections have to be admitted. It might be argued, for instance, that no one could say he wanted a Scottish Parliament unless he knew what kind of Scottish Parliament was being offered to him. Yet it is impossible to deny, in view of the success of the Covenant, that there is a widespread desire in Scotland today for some form of devolution within the framework of the United Kingdom. The Government do not want to sponsor a plebiscite, for it would probably produce the evidence that was least welcome to them. They do not even desire to have a full enquiry into the whole question. Their motto seems to be "Let sleeping dogs lie". Only this, as it happens, is not a sleeping dog.

In decrying the demand for devolution it is grossly unfair to judge the strength of that demand, as some do, by the failure of Scottish Nationalist candidates at a General Election. It is unfair, because, in general, these candidates stand for complete separation from England and, secondly, because moderate Scottish opinion recognises that at a General Election, in such troubled times as these, there are greater issues. It would seem, therefore, desirable that the National Covenant Committee should devote some part of the funds which they have been collecting to the holding of an unofficial plebiscite. The Government will not sponsor one, even if only for information. It must therefore be held, if at all, under private auspices, as the Kirriemuir plebiscite was. Its validity as an indication of opinion would depend not only on the generality of the response to it, but also upon the way in which the questions were framed, and that would require careful thought. If the result favoured devolution the Government would doubtless accuse the voters of ignorance of the issues involved, but they are themselves apparently determined not to throw too much light on these issues if one may judge by the limited character of the inquiry they have inaugurated.

(c) *Leading Article published in the* Scotsman *on 9th August, 1950*

Both of the major parties have rejected the National Covenant Committee's claim for a plebiscite on Scottish self-government. Mr. McNeil stated the Government's view last week, and the Unionist attitude is expressed in correspondence published yesterday. The Government even shirked the question whether the Scottish people were entitled to have a Parliament, if they clearly showed their desire for one.

The Unionists agree that if the people of Scotland were ultimately to decide in favour of a Parliament no one could gainsay them. But the point is, what evidence will be accepted as convincing proof that the majority of the people desire self-government. The Covenant Committee can argue that the result of the local poll in Kirriemuir, and, still more, the 1,600,000 signatures attached to the Covenant testify to the widespread support for devolution within the framework of the United Kingdom. If that is not regarded as a clear enough manifestation of the popular will, they reasonably suggest that public opinion should be further tested by means of a plebiscite. For similar reasons both parties will have nothing to do with a referendum. They say that complex constitutional matters should not be settled by a plebiscite, and that such changes can be made only by the normal processes of Parliamentary democracy.

In his reply to the Unionist letter Mr. John MacCormick acutely analyses the illogical position of the main parties. They imply that the desire for self-government should be demonstrated by voters at an election. When an election takes place, however, they claim that larger issues are at stake, which overshadow the minor domestic problems of Scotland and urge the electors to ignore the latter. Self-government is a complex matter, but electors could surely express a more reasoned opinion on it if it were presented in isolation in the form of a plebiscite than if it were submerged by other complex issues at an election. Voters nowadays express a general preference for one party; their decision is seldom based on support for one particular item in the programme.

It is not clear what degree of electoral success the parties would accept as proof of the reality of the desire for self-government. Would it be enough, if a majority of successful Scottish candidates pledged themselves to support it? Such pledges are apt to be forgotten, as we have learned since 1945. Could self-government be granted, only if a majority in the British Parliament were in favour of it? In other words, must the movement be frustrated, unless it is adopted by one of the major parties? By denying the Scottish people an opportunity of giving a plain answer to a question that cuts across party loyalties the Socialist and Unionist leaders run the risk of encouraging the growth of extremism. The Covenant Movement, Mr. Ivor Brown writes elsewhere in our columns, is essentially sober and moderate; it is sheer misrepresentation to accuse it of separatism. But, if reasonable demands are rejected and the Scottish people are denied an opportunity of expressing their views, except through the existing party machinery in which English influence is naturally predominant, they may become exasperated and persuaded that they will gain a hearing only if they make a nuisance of themselves. The form of Scottish government should be settled in a calm and amicable manner, but the obstructive attitude of the parties may compel the Covenant movement, as Mr. Brown suggests, to reconsider its strategy.

APPENDIX THREE

Excerpt from Opinion by Lord Cooper,
Lord President of the Court of Session in the
Queen's Title Action
(MacCormick and Another v. Lord Advocate, 1953)

THE PROCLAMATION issued on 28th May, 1953, in pursuance of the Act of 1953 substitutes Northern Ireland for Ireland alters the formula applicable to the Commonwealth and Empire overseas; but leaves the name and the numeral and the rest of the style and title unaffected. I find it impossible to hold that the Act of 1953 authorised, either retrospectively or by anticipation, the adoption by Her Majesty of the name and numeral by which she was initially proclaimed and has ever since been officially known.

I interpose the observation that, if it were necessary to construe the Act of 1953, I should find it impossible to do so because the Act is not self contained. All the other Acts dealing with a change in the Royal Style and Titles simply authorised the Sovereign to adopt such changed styles and titles as the sovereign might think fit. But in 1953 the sovereign's discretion in the matter is not unqualified. The changed styles and titles to which Parliament assented must be such as Her Majesty may think fit *"having regard to the said Agreement"*. What Agreement? Plainly the Agreement said to have been concluded with the Dominion representatives in 1952. But this Agreement is not scheduled or otherwise detailed, the only reference to it being in the vague words of the preamble of the Act, which are entirely lacking in specification. The Lord Advocate admitted that the Act was not self-explanatory, and offered in supplement a White Paper, which he indicated had been made available in the Vote Office prior to the consideration of the Bill. But Parliament can only speak through the medium of a statute. A Court of Law is not entitled to investigate the Parliamentary History of a Bill whether in the pages of Hansard or their equivalent a "white paper", and I am therefore forced to the conclusion that this act must remain incapable of being fully understood or intelligently interpreted by any Court, the legislature having withheld the material necessary for that purpose. Be that as it may. I consider that the Lord Advocate failed to show that there is or ever was, Parliamentary authority for the adoption by Her Majesty of the name and the "numeral" which in fact were adopted on Her Majesty's Accession and have been used ever since.

Upon this view a part of the Lord Ordinary's judgement and of the argument before us disappears. But lest this case should go further I shall briefly express my opinion.

The principle of the unlimited Sovereignty of Parliament is a distinctively English principle which has no counterpart in Scottish Constitutional law. It derives its origin from Coke and Blackstone, and was widely popularised during the eighteenth century by Bagehot and Dicey, the latter having stated the doctrine in its classic form in his *Constitutional Law*. Considering that the Union legislation extinguished the Parliaments of Scotland and England, and replaced them by a new Parliament, I have difficulty in seeing why it should have been supposed that the new Parliament of Great Britain must inherit all the peculiar characteristics of the English Parliament but none of the Scottish Parliament, as if all that happened in 1707 was that Scottish representatives were admitted to the Parliament of England. That is not what was done. Further the Treaty and the associated legislation, by which the Parliament of Great Britain was brought into being, as the successor of the separate Parliaments of Scotland and England, contain some clauses which expressly reserve to the Parliament of Great Britain powers of subsequent modification, and other clauses which either contain no such power or emphatically exclude subsequent alteration by declaration that the provisions shall be fundamental and unalterable in all time coming, or declarations of a like effect. I have never been able to understand how it is possible to reconcile with elementary canons of construction the adoption by the English Constitutional theorists of the same attitude to those materially different types of provisions.

The Lord Advocate conceded this point by admitting that the Parliament of Great Britain "could not" repeal or alter such "fundamental and essential" conditions. He was doubtless influenced in making this concession by the modified views expressed by Dicey in his later work entitled *Thoughts on the Scottish Union*, from which I take this passage (pp. 252-3): "The statesmen of 1707, though giving full sovereign power to the Parliament of Great Britain clearly believed in the possibility of creating an absolute sovereign legislature which should yet be bound by unalterable laws." After instancing the provisions as to Presbyterian Church government in Scotland with their emphatic prohibition against alteration, the author proceeds: "It represents the conviction of the Parliament which passed the Act of Union that the Act for the Security of the Church of Scotland ought to be morally or constitutionally unchangeable even by the British Parliament. . . . A Sovereign Parliament in short, though it cannot be logically bound to abstain from changing any given law, may by the fact that an Act when it was passed had been declared to be unchangeable, receive a warning that it cannot be changed without grave danger to the constitution of the country."

I have not found in the Union Legislation any provision

that the Parliament of Great Britain should be absolutely
sovereign in the sense that Parliament should be free to alter
the Treaty at will. However that may be, these passages
provide a necessary corrective to the extreme formulations
adopted by the Lord Ordinary, and not now supported. In
the latest editions of the *Constitutional Law* the editor
uneasily described Dicey's theories as "purely lawyers'
conceptions" and demonstrates how deeply later events,
such as the Statute of Westminster, have encroached upon
the earlier dogma. As is well known the conflict between
academic logic and political reality has been emphasised
by the recent South African decision as to the effect of the
Statute of Westminster (*Harris* v. *Minister of Interior*, 1952,
1 T.L.R. 1245).

But the Petitioners have still a grave difficulty to overcome
on this branch of their argument. Accepting it that there
are provisions in the Treaty of Union and associated legislation which are "fundamental law" and assuming for the
moment that something is alleged to have been done—it
matters not whether with legislative authority or not—in
breach of that fundamental law, the question remains
whether such a question is determinable as a justifiable
issue in the Courts of either Scotland or England in the same
fashion as an issue of Constitutional *vires* would be cognisable
by the Supreme Courts of the United States, or of South
Africa or Australia. I reserve my opinion with regard to the
provisions relating expressly to this court and to the laws
"which concern private right" which are administered here.
This is not such a question, but a matter of "public right"
(Articles XVIII and XIX). To put the matter in another
way it is of little avail to ask whether the Parliament of
Great Britain can do this thing or that, without going on to
enquire who can stop them if they do. Any person *can*
repudiate his solemn engagement but he cannot normally

do so with impunity. Only two answers have been suggested to this corollary to the main question. The first is the exceedingly cynical answer implied by Dicey (*Constitutional Law*, p. 82) in the statement that "It would be rash of the Imperial Parliament to abolish the Scotch Courts and assimilate the Law of Scotland to that of England. But no one can feel sure at what point Scottish resistance to such a change would become serious." The other answer was that nowadays there may be room for the invocation of an "advisory opinion" from the International Court of Justice. On these matters I express no view.

APPENDIX FOUR

Why a National Party? –
John MacCormick's view in 1928, addressed to his future wife.

Thesis: That the National Party of Scotland is the only medium through which Scotland can (a) gain self-government and (b) rebuild her social, economic and cultural life.

Addressed to Miss Margaret Isobel Miller.

Warning:- This is not a literary endeavour; I am simply talking to you – (but you can't interrupt!)

May I presume, Margaret, that there is no need to bore you with all the facts and figures which show that under English Government, Scotland's industry, agriculture and social development are almost entirely neglected? I shall proceed throughout on the hypothesis that you believe self-government to be a worthy object and have doubts only over how it should be achieved, or its urgency.

I think it best to take the prosaic arguments first. Later on I shall approach the subject from the more personal point of view and give you, as far as I can, a history of my own progress to my present point of view.

If you consider self-government to be an urgent need then I think the only ground on which you can attack the National Party is this: that since the Labour Party is already pledged to satisfy that need, the existence of the new party will hamper instead of help the progress of the cause.

Now I think it is very easy to show that, in spite of its pledges, the Labour Party is very unlikely to put through any considerable measure of self government. Like the Liberal Party in days gone by it will find, whenever it attains a majority in the House of Commons, that if it loses its Scots Members it also loses its majority; and no party can reasonably be trusted to do anything that will rob it of its power to govern. The most that can be expected of the Labour Party when it comes into power is the passing of some devolution scheme which will set up in Scotland a subsidiary Parliament (really a magnified Town Council) and will still maintain Scottish representation more or less on the present basis in the English Chamber. This, indeed, is all that the leaders of the Labour Party have ever pledged themselves to, and in my opinion such a scheme is to be feared even more than the continuance of the present regime.

Scotland would be in the same position as Northern Ireland. She would have to pay a double set of taxes, and to maintain the expense of a double system of elections; she would still, to a large extent, be controlled by the English Parties; she would be in continual doubt as to the exact limit of her powers and at the same time she would still be bound willy-nilly to the Imperialistic foreign policy of England. But worst of all, her position would be such that very little could be done to improve it; for if "Home Rule" has been granted, anyone who cries out for something more will be in grave danger of being condemned as a crank or a fool.

So much then for the Labour Party's pledge. But you may say, are not other things even more urgently needed than self-government, such as proper housing, better industrial conditions etc., and could not the Labour Party, if it attained power, attend to these things while Scotland is still in her present position? I very much doubt it! In the first place leaders of the Labour Party are openly convinced that these things can only come about by a gradual process extending over many decades. My own conviction is the very opposite.

I believe that it is only by the sudden uprising of some tremendous human sentiment (such as patriotism) that we can ever rid ourselves of the degradation of poverty and wasted life that is our shame today. It *must* be a sudden process, for unless humanity is on the crest of the wave of some great enthusiasm I am afraid it is all too content to slide along in the groove of daily use and wont. I believe that is sound psychology.

It is my hope that the National Party, by stirring up and wisely directing the patriotism of the Scottish people, will be able to accomplish in a very short time what would otherwise take many years.

Again I must criticise the Labour Party on another ground, namely its actual composition. As you well know, it is for the most part an agglomeration of Trade Unions. Now, in my fairly intimate contact with the Labour Party, I discovered that the average Trade Unionist has a very restricted outlook: in other words he is usually a very 'sectionally' minded man. Let me take a recent example of the effects of this. The town of Sheffield (I think it was Sheffield) applied to Parliament a few months ago for powers to run buses in and around the city. This, of course, was a definite step towards Socialism, but Mr J.H. Thomas and the other railwaymen in Parliament opposed the measure on the instructions of their Union, which feared that the development of municipal motor transport systems would be a serious menace to the prosperity of the Railways.

I believe that only a party whose view is nation-wide can succeed in rebuilding the structure of our social life.

Perhaps you will say I am devoting too much attention to the Labour Party? Well I know it best but I believe that to an even greater extent what I say of it applies to the other two parties.

Well Margaret, I think we'll get down to personalities

now. Why did I take up this business of the National Party? I shall report briefly the first conversation in which I ever gave voice to the conclusions of that fairly long and serious meditation which led to my leaving the Labour Party. The participants were Jim Valentine, Fergus Rodger, and myself. We were discussing things in general over a coffee in the Keir Hardie Institute (I regard the occasion as historical because that talk gave birth to the Scottish Nationalist Association and that led to – well – !), I forget the context, but at any rate our discussion centred round democracy in general and the party system in particular. I had been in the I.L.P. for about two years and had found myself growing increasingly unsympathetic with its atmosphere. Of course, it was only my own personal feeling but I thought there was far too much dogmatism, too much self-righteousness about it. Everything was wrong that wasn't I.L.P.–ism. There was not the slightest possibility of anything else being right. Now I don't think I boast when I say that to my nature such an attitude of mind is very distasteful. I cannot but think that nothing is finally and absolutely true, just as nothing is completely false. That is my nature and I cannot help it.

I was expressing my discontent to my friends; I was complaining that democracy, as manipulated by the Party System, must always be very slow moving in a forward direction; I was bemoaning the fact that such highly intelligent young men as ourselves (!) could take no part in trying to improve the world without tying ourselves up in a Party which would demand from us a very strict and very irksome obedience. And I believe I expressed a wish that we could more or less create a party of our own which would express our ideals and, to some extent, be subject to our control. From that point it was but a short step to the Scottish Nationalist Association and the National Party of Scotland. I may say that we discussed the formation of that

Party without knowing in the least that, even at that time, other organisations were feeling their way towards the idea.

I going to become very intimate, Margaret, but before I go any further I want to assure you of the utter sincerity of my position in the National Party. Largely I believe, because of my own way of talking, a good many people imagine that I have only taken up the matter either for fun or for notoriety. I hate prating about sincerity but you will realise how much I want you to believe that I am convinced that the National Party is the best possible instrument for the building up of a better and more just form of society. All personal ambitions aside (and of course I have these), if I did not think that I should have nothing to do with it.

What I have to say now I have never said to anyone else and I find it difficult to say even to you, but I want to very much and I know that you will understand me. Margaret, you have often asked me what I am going to be, and I have often replied vaguely simply because I am sometimes astounded (even terrified) by my own ambitions. It is not so much what I want to *be* as what I want to *do*, and what deep down in me I am convinced I *can* do. This must seem terrible in writing but I am speaking out-right simply because I feel that already you are somehow part of me, and I of you. I must speak to you as I do to myself.

I want to turn things completely about in this sorry world of ours. I want to make Scotland as near a Utopia as is humanly possible. I don't believe this can ever be attempted by the ordinary methods of democratic government, which are well enough suited for administration but ill adapted to creation. I want to win for myself the power of a free hand, and the National Party is the first step on the way.

John

INDEX